The Validity of Gains in Scores on the Kentucky Instructional Results Information System (KIRIS)

Daniel M. Koretz

Sheila I. Barron

RAND Education

RAND

The research described in this report was supported by RAND Education with funding by Grant 94-002248-000 from The Pew Charitable Trust, and Grant 960-0402 from The Ford Foundation. The conclusions reported here, however, are solely those of the authors and do not represent positions of The Pew Charitable Trusts or The Ford Foundation.

ISBN: 0-8330-2687-9

Building on more than 25 years of research and evaluation work, RAND Education (formerly RAND's Institute on Education and Training) has as its mission the improvement of educational policy and practice in formal and informal settings from early childhood on. RAND is a nonprofit institution that helps improve policy and decisionmaking through research and analysis. RAND® is a registered trademark. RAND's publications do not necessarily reflect the opinions or policies of its research sponsors.

Published 1998 by RAND
1700 Main Street, P.O. Box 2138, Santa Monica, CA 90407-2138
1333 H St., N.W., Washington, D.C. 20005-4707
RAND URL: http://www.rand.org/
To order RAND documents or to obtain additional information, contact Distribution Services: Telephone: (310) 451-7002; Fax: (310) 451-6915; Internet: order@rand.org

PREFACE

In recent years, many states and localities have attempted to improve the performance of schools and increase the learning of students by holding educators or students accountable for students' scores on assessments of achievement. In the 1970s, this approach often took the form of requiring that students pass relatively easy, minimum-competency tests. In the 1980s, that approach was often supplanted by or supplemented with a program that held educators accountable for scores on standardized, norm-referenced multiple-choice tests.

When teachers tailor their teaching too closely to these assessments, however, instruction can be degraded, and scores can become inflated as students focus unduly on the specific content of the tests rather than focusing on the broad domains of achievement the tests are intended to represent. Spurred by a growing awareness of these problems, policymakers over the past decade have increasingly used other forms of assessment in educational accountability programs, in the hopes that these will be "worth teaching to." They have used a variety of forms of performance assessment, including essays, hands-on performance tasks, portfolios, and group tasks. One of the archetypes of this new wave of assessment-based reform was the Kentucky Instructional Results Information System (KIRIS). KIRIS assigned rewards and sanctions to schools largely on the basis of trends in scores on a complex, partially performance-based assessment.

Despite widespread enthusiasm for this new direction in assessment-based accountability, it is far from certain that it will avoid the problems that have arisen with accountability using traditional, multiple-choice tests. For example, there are no technical reasons to assume that performance assessments will be immune to the problem of inflated scores.

Accordingly, with support from The Pew Charitable Trusts and The Ford Foundation, RAND undertook an evaluation of the KIRIS system. An earlier study (Koretz, Barron, Mitchell, and Stecher, 1996) reported evidence pertaining to the effects of the program on schooling. This report presents an evaluation of the large gains in scores observed over the first years of the KIRIS program. That is, it evaluates the degree to which these gains in scores indicate that student learning improved.

CONTENTS

FIGURES

TABLES

SUMMARY

Kentucky's education reform program, named KERA after the Kentucky Education Reform Act from which it emanated, has been one of the most influential statewide reform programs of the 1990s. It has entailed a systemic overhaul of Kentucky's K-12 educational system but has been best known for the assessment and accountability system it put into place. This system—the Kentucky Instructional Results Information System (KIRIS)—has assigned rewards and sanctions to schools largely on the basis of trends in scores on the complex, partially performance-based KIRIS assessment. KIRIS has become one of the archetypes in the national debate about standards-based accountability systems.

Scores on the KIRIS assessment, along with other variables such as dropout rates that were given much less weight, were combined into an accountability index for each school. Scores on the accountability index were reported annually, but schools were formally evaluated on the basis of changes over a two-year period. Each school was assigned a performance target based on its index averaged over the first two years of an accountability cycle. Schools that exceeded their targets for the next two-year average by a sufficient margin were given cash rewards; those that fell below the target by a sufficient amount were sanctioned. The curricular guidelines that accompanied the assessment were initially very vague, although they were gradually made somewhat more specific.

Large gains in scores on the KIRIS assessment soon resulted, and these were presented by proponents of the KERA program as an indication of success. The meaning of these increases, however, is not clear. Scores on high-stakes tests can increase substantially more than actual improvements in student learning warrant. This inflation of score gains, which creates an illusion of success, can arise from numerous factors, such as familiarization with the assessment and inappropriate teaching to the test. Research has shown that the inflation of scores can be large in systems that hold educators responsible for scores on traditional, multiple-choice tests, and indeed, the recognition of this risk was one of many factors that gave impetus to the current wave of performance-based testing. The extent of inflation of scores on large-scale performance-based assessments, however, has been subject to little research.

Two previous studies suggested the possibility that KIRIS score gains might be appreciably inflated. A committee empaneled by the Kentucky General Assembly noted that while fourth-grade KIRIS reading scores increased dramatically between 1992 and 1994, Kentucky's fourth-grade reading scores on the National Assessment of Educational Progress (NAEP) remained essentially unchanged. Similarly, over the same period, the KIRIS mathematics and reading scores of twelfth-grade students who also took the American College Testing (ACT) college-admissions tests increased substantially, while their ACT mathematics and reading scores did not change. The committee concluded that "gains in KIRIS scores [were] substantially inflated [between 1992 and 1994] and provide the public with a misleading view of improvements in student performance" (Hambleton, et al., 1995, p. 8-4). A survey of representative samples of fourth- and eighth-grade Kentucky educators about their responses to KIRIS also found reason to suspect that gains might be inflated. Educators reported making instructional changes consonant with the goals of KERA, but many also reported relying on test preparation and de-emphasizing untested content. Perhaps most important, only a small minority attributed the gains in their schools to improvements in knowledge and skills; many more attributed them to test preparation and familiarization with the assessment (Koretz, Barron, Mitchell, and Stecher, 1996).

Accordingly, this study was undertaken to explore the validity of the observed gains in scores on KIRIS—that is, to evaluate the extent to which they justify the inference that student learning has improved. It examines performance starting with the first administration of the KIRIS assessment in the spring of 1992 and continuing through the 1995 and 1996 administrations. We used both *external* evidence of validity (evidence provided by other assessments) and *internal* evidence of validity (evidence offered by patterns of performance on KIRIS itself). The external evidence included fourth-grade mathematics trends on NAEP and more recent ACT data than those used by Hambleton, et al. (1995). Performance changes in 1997 are described but not analyzed in detail. Although KIRIS assesses students in numerous subjects, this study focused primarily on mathematics, reading, and science, the three subjects that offered the best external evidence.

The composition of the KIRIS assessment changed repeatedly over the period we examined. Multiple-choice items, "performance events" (complex performances that entailed group as well as individual activities), and mathematics portfolios were included in the accountability index in some years but not others. Our study focused on the open-response portion of the "transitional" assessment, which is the one portion of the assessment that was included in the accountability index every year.

Traditional methods of validation focus primarily on cross-sectional evidence—that is, evidence about the quality of information from an assessment at any one point in time. Such evidence is necessary but insufficient for evaluating the validity of *changes* in scores over time. Accordingly, cross-sectional validity evidence is cited where germane but was not the focus of this study.

A FRAMEWORK FOR EVALUATING GAINS ON KIRIS

Validity is an attribute of a particular inference based on a score, not of the score itself. Thus the validity of gains on KIRIS hinges in part on the inferences that users base on them. For example, if users present (or interpret) increases in KIRIS mathematics scores as indicating improved mastery of a broadly defined domain of mathematics, then one would expect true gains in student learning to produce some echo of KIRIS gains in scores on other assessments of similar mathematical domains. But if users interpret KIRIS gains as indicating improved mastery of unusual aspects of mathematics not commonly assessed by other tests, then valid gains on KIRIS might be reflected by little or no increase in scores on other tests.

What this means for KIRIS can be illustrated using NAEP, whose frameworks were a model for the KIRIS frameworks. Observed gains on KIRIS in mathematics can be seen as comprising three components of unknown size: (1) meaningful gains that should generalize to NAEP because of similarities between the assessments; (2) meaningful gains that may not generalize well to NAEP because of idiosyncratic aspects of KIRIS; and (3) inflation of KIRIS scores. The size of gains on NAEP in Kentucky provides an upper-bound estimate of the first of these components, but the split between the second and third components depends on the interpretation given to gains.

It is important to note that inflation of gains can stem from many sources and need not imply that scores become less meaningful over time. For example, if students' lack of familiarity with the demands of an assessment initially causes them to score more poorly on it than their level of proficiency warrants, their scores may rise over time as they come to understand the assessment's demands better. In that case, later scores may be more accurate than initial scores, but even in that case, the *gain* in score would be misleadingly large. In many cases, however, inflation of gains will arise because scores become increasingly misleading over time. This can happen, for example, if teachers increasingly focus their instruction on the specific demands of the assessment at the cost of lessened emphasis on other important aspects of the domain the test is intended to represent.

TRENDS IN KIRIS SCORES

During the period we studied, KIRIS scores were reported on a categorical scale with four points: Novice, Apprentice, Proficient, and Distinguished. These were arbitrarily assigned scores of 0, 40, 100, and 140 by the Kentucky Department of Education (KDE). For purposes of our study, KIRIS scores were standardized, and changes were expressed as fractions of a standard deviation.[1]

The performance targets for schools were set arbitrarily, without information on actual patterns of school performance. Regardless of their starting points, all schools were expected to reach a mean score of 100 on the accountability index—equivalent to having all students performing at the Proficient level—at the end of 20 years. Thus, in terms of the index, lower-performing schools were expected to make larger gains.

Actual data on student performance show that the gains required of most schools were very large. To meet expectations, a typical school would have had to show improvement of roughly 2 standard deviations over the 20 years, or 0.2 standard deviation per year. The increases needed to obtain rewards were of course larger. By any standard, these expected gains are very large. For example, on most tests, the much discussed achievement decline of the 1960s and 1970s was less than 0.4 standard deviation in total. The mean difference in eighth-grade mathematics between the U.S. and Japan (one of the highest-scoring countries) in the Third International Mathematics and Science Study (TIMSS) was roughly 1 standard deviation.

---

[1]The complications inherent in standardizing this scale and the methods used to address them are described in the Appendix as well as in the body of the report.

Many schools met or exceeded these very high expectations during the first years of the program, producing many large average gains for the state as a whole. For example, between 1992 and 1993, the statewide mean in reading increased by 1.3 standard deviations, and the gains in mathematics and science were 0.6 and 0.5 standard deviation. The gains in the secondary grades were smaller but nonetheless generally very large. For example, in the eighth grade, the average score increased by 0.6 standard deviation in mathematics and by roughly 0.4 standard deviation in reading and science. The simple size of the larger of the KIRIS gains raises questions about validity.

RETENTION IN GRADE

Trends in test scores can be distorted by changes in the test-taking population. The design of KIRIS—which required that almost all students be tested and which assigned scores of zero to students not tested—removed much of the potential for biases of this sort. It would still be possible, however, for schools to raise scores artificially by holding low-performing students back in grade before they reached the grades in which KIRIS was administered.

To evaluate this potential threat to the validity of gains, we examined changes in the age distribution of tested students through 1995. We found no evidence of changes that might contribute to inflated scores. Indeed, the one appreciable change we found, a modest decrease in the age of students tested in the fourth grade, would lessen gains in scores.

EXTERNAL EVIDENCE FROM NAEP

No state-representative NAEP data in reading are available beyond those reported by Hambleton, et al. (1995). Mathematics data, however, are available for the period 1992 through 1996 in both the fourth and eighth grades. These data are a particularly important form of external evidence because the KIRIS assessment frameworks were explicitly linked to those of NAEP. The first KIRIS technical report stated that "the [Kentucky] valued outcomes, as supplemented by frameworks from the National Assessment of Educational Progress (NAEP), will determine what is to be assessed and how it is to be assessed. . . . Using the NAEP frameworks as a supplement to the valued outcomes also ensured that the Kentucky tests could be compared to NAEP. . . . Kentucky's reading framework [is] similar to that of the 1992 NAEP framework. . . . The entire [mathematics] framework is consistent with the most recent NAEP framework for mathematics" (Kentucky Department of Education, 1993a, pp. 4, 14, 17). Given this clear linkage, meaningful gains on KIRIS—that is, gains that reflect increased mastery of the domains specified in the frameworks—should be reflected to a substantial degree in scores on NAEP.

During the years in question, the NAEP mathematics scores of Kentucky students did increase by a considerable amount (by 0.17 standard deviation in the fourth grade and 0.13 standard deviation in the eighth grade). Gains on KIRIS, however, were far larger: roughly 3.6 times as large in the fourth grade and 4.1 times as large in the eighth grade. Even allowing for substantial differences between the two assessments, this large a disparity between the two trends would suggest that the KIRIS gains were considerably inflated.

The increases on NAEP in Kentucky may have been a reflection of a broad national trend rather than an echo of specific responses to KERA. Kentucky's increases on NAEP were similar to the national average, and most states for which there are representative data showed increases quite similar to Kentucky's.

EXTERNAL EVIDENCE FROM THE ACT

The ACT is less valuable than NAEP as external evidence for several reasons. Its frameworks are less similar to those of KIRIS, it includes only multiple-choice items, and it is taken by an unrepresentative sample of the state's high school students.

However, there are reasons to expect that KIRIS gains should be echoed on the ACT, even if perhaps less so than on NAEP. The sample of students taking the ACT constitutes roughly half of the eleventh-grade student population, and their trends on KIRIS have been reasonably similar to those in the state as a whole. The content of the assessments shows a considerable degree of overlap, and scores on the two assessments have been moderately highly correlated. Therefore, KDE argued that the correlations between KIRIS and the ACT provide concurrent evidence of the validity of KIRIS and wrote: "Fortunately, as shown in the KIRIS Accountability Cycle I Technical Manual, there is significant correlation between KIRIS and ACT scores, and *it is not overly presumptuous to assume that increased learning that leads to improvement on one is likely to lead to improvement on the other*" (Kentucky Department of Education, 1997, p. 14-7, emphasis added).

Between 1992 and 1995, the KIRIS gains of high school students in reading and mathematics were not reflected at all in their ACT scores. In mathematics, the contrast was striking, a difference of about 0.7 standard deviation. The difference in reading was about 0.4 standard deviation. In science, ACT scores increased by a modest 0.1 standard deviation, while KIRIS scores increased about five times as much. This would seem clear evidence of appreciable inflation of gains in reading and especially in mathematics. The interpretation of the science trends is complicated by the concurrent but smaller increase on the ACT. Even allowing for more substantial differences between the ACT and KIRIS than between NAEP and KIRIS, however, trend disparities this large suggest appreciable inflation of gains on KIRIS.

INTERNAL EVIDENCE FROM KIRIS

The fact that many KIRIS items are reused from one year to the next could provide, in theory, a basis for evaluating the validity of gains. For example, if the difference between performance on new and reused items is larger in high-gain schools than in low-gain schools, one possible explanation would be test preparation that inflated gains by focusing inappropriately on reused test items.

In practice, however, our analysis of internal evidence pertaining to the validity of KIRIS gains was limited by numerous factors. The methods used by KDE to link scores from one year to the next did not produce clear estimates of the relative difficulty of new and reused items. Changes in the assessment from year to year may have distorted changes in item-level performance, and relatively few reused items were free of such possible confoundings. In addition, methods for using internal evidence to validate gains in scores are poorly developed.

We conducted analyses of internal evidence for reading and mathematics. Because of their complexity, some of these were limited to two cases that showed relatively large gains: fourth-grade reading and eighth-grade mathematics from 1994 to 1995.

The internal evidence in mathematics was generally consistent with some inflation of scores, although there were some exceptions, and some of the differences analyzed were small. Students found new items harder than reused ones by a small margin in grade 4 and by more substantial amounts in grade 8. All reused mathematics item sets examined showed score increases over time. When these two changes were combined, the result in most instances was a "sawtooth" pattern in which item performance increased when items were reused but dropped again when new items were introduced. The discrepancy in performance on new versus reused items tended to be greater in schools that showed larger overall gains in KIRIS mathematics scores. This relationship, while modest, would be consistent with coaching focused on reused items that could inflate scores.

The results for reading were less consistent. In both grades, students found new reading items more difficult than reused ones in only one year (1994) of those considered. In most sets of reused reading items, however, performance did increase over time, leading to a sawtooth pattern that had a number of exceptions. Perhaps more important, the association between score gains and the difference in performance on new versus reused items that appeared in mathematics was absent in reading.

CONCLUSIONS AND IMPLICATIONS

Taken together, the internal evidence and external evidence suggest inflation of score gains in mathematics. They also suggest a mechanism—item-specific coaching tailored to reused items—that may have contributed to it. The size of the inflation cannot be estimated precisely, but given certain assumptions about the inferences users base on KIRIS scores, the exaggeration of gains would appear to be appreciable. The evidence is less clear-cut in reading. Some of the gains in reading were particularly implausible, and the external evidence is consistent with inflation. The external evidence is more limited in reading than in mathematics, however, and the internal evidence is less consistent.

An important caveat is that most of these findings reflect only the four years following the first administration of KIRIS in 1992. Large initial gains are common when new assessments are implemented, and other research has shown that these initial gains do not always generalize well enough to constitute evidence of real gains in student learning. Familiarization with the demands of the new assessment often underlies some of these initial gains. It is important to note that familiarization may in some cases increase the validity of scores, but even then it can exaggerate—that is, decrease the validity of—*gains* in scores.

Given that initial gains from familiarization are common, four years may be too short a time to evaluate the effects of an assessment such as KIRIS. But given the uses to which scores were put, it is not too short a time to validate gains. As is routine in the case of large-scale assessments, KDE presented the initial gains in scores to educators and the public as clear evidence of large improvements in performance; in addition, the Department awarded tens of millions of dollars in rewards to schools on the basis of these gains. Thus, it is essential to ask whether these inferences were warranted—that is, to evaluate the validity of gains.

An alternative way to address the problem of initial familiarization would be for sponsors of new assessments to advise educators and the public to discount gains over the first years of the program and to avoid using initial gains as evidence of improved student performance. If sponsors were to take these steps, and if users (including the press) were to follow suit, the meaningfulness of initial score gains would be less an issue. We are not aware, however, of any instances in which the sponsors of large-scale high-stakes assessments have taken these steps.

In the absence of systematic research documenting test-based accountability systems that have avoided the problem of inflated gains, one can only speculate about how best to alleviate this problem in the future. Several steps, however, may be helpful:

- *Set realistic goals for the improvement of performance.* If teachers are told that they must make larger and more rapid gains in scores than they can accomplish by legitimate means, they will have a greater incentive to cut corners by teaching to the test in ways that will inflate gains.
- *Tie assessments to clear curricula.* If teachers are to improve performance on the domain a test is supposed to represent, rather than only on the sample included in the test itself, they must be given a clear understanding of what the domain is. If teachers are confronted with a centralized testing program but given no accompanying curriculum, they will have a strong incentive to use the test as a surrogate curriculum framework, increasing the risk of narrowed instruction and inflated gains.
- *Design assessments to minimize inflation.* Most assessment designs represent a trade-off between various measurement and practical goals. Using a test for accountability may change the balance among these competing goals and may require that steps be taken to minimize inflation. Sampling systematically from specified domains may be necessary to avoid narrowed instruction, for example, and limiting the reuse of items may be necessary to lessen the potential impact of certain types of coaching.
- *Monitor for potential inflation of gains.* Score inflation is a great enough risk that test-based accountability systems should often be designed to monitor for its possibility. Such monitoring could involve external audit testing, adaptations to the testing program itself, or both.
- *Credit other aspects of educational performance.* Since the amount of protection against score inflation that can be obtained by improving the design of assessment programs is unknown, and assessments usually measure only a subset of valued educational outcomes, improvements to large-scale assessment programs may be insufficient. The goal of improved student performance may

also require accountability systems that take into account shorter-term outcomes and perhaps the quality of practice itself.

This study also illustrated in numerous ways the limitations of current research on the validity of gains. As long as test-based accountability systems remain popular, it will be important to improve the tools that can be brought to bear on this issue. Research on the validity of gains might be strengthened by refinements in assessment design, by further development of analytical methods, and by accompanying research on scores with investigations of the mechanisms that underlie score inflation.

Finally, it is important to place the results of this study in context. Policymakers in Kentucky have been embroiled in controversy over KIRIS for some time, and the Kentucky General Assembly recently enacted legislation that will bring about major changes to the KIRIS testing and accountability system. While the findings reported here are relevant to that debate, to view them as specific to Kentucky would be to lose an opportunity. KIRIS has embodied themes common in educational reform programs nationwide, and the experience with KIRIS holds lessons for other programs as well.

ACKNOWLEDGMENTS

We would like to acknowledge the help of the many people who assisted in this effort. Without the aid of numerous people at the Kentucky Department of Education, this study would not have been possible. Ed Reidy, then Deputy Commissioner of Education in Kentucky, insisted that the Kentucky assessment system be open to outside scrutiny and facilitated this study of KIRIS as well as numerous others. Both Brian Gong and Scott Trimble offered important assistance. We owe particular thanks to Jonathan Dings. We often needed to call on his extensive knowledge of the technical aspects of KIRIS, and he was generous with his time and expertise.

Bob Ziomek at American College Testing provided data, documentation, and explanations that were needed for our comparisons of ACT and KIRIS trends. John Mazzeo at the Educational Testing Service provided information and data pertaining to NAEP. Several people at RAND also deserve our thanks. Dan McCaffrey provided statistical consulting; Tom Sullivan and Laurie MacDonald carried out much of the statistical programming. Gina Schuyler, the project's research assistant, carried out innumerable tasks with patience and diligence, including creating from many sources an intricate database that tracked the use, placement, and editing of KIRIS items and rubrics across all grades, subjects, and years. Detailed and thoughtful reviews were provided by Brian Stecher and Larry Hanser of RAND, Jonathan Dings of the Kentucky Department of Education, and Laurie Wise of the Human Resources Research Organization.

While these individuals helped in many, invaluable ways, they are blameless for any errors of fact or interpretation in this report.

1. INTRODUCTION

Kentucky's educational reform program, named KERA for the Kentucky Education Reform Act from which it emanated, is one of the most prominent and influential standards-based reform efforts in the nation. KERA has entailed a thorough overhaul of the state's K-12 educational system. It has altered, for example, the financing of schools, the organization of primary grades (instituting a statewide ungraded primary program), professional development, the governance of schools, and the state's assessment program, and it instituted a statewide program of school-level accountability for performance.

Despite its scope, KERA is known outside the state primarily because of its assessment and accountability system—the Kentucky Instructional Results Information System (KIRIS). This system used a complex, partially performance-based assessment, in conjunction with noncognitive indicators such as dropout rates that are given less weight, to judge the performance of schools. Scores were reported annually, but schools were evaluated every two years on the basis of changes in performance from one two-year average to the next.[1] These periods were called *bienniums* or *accountability cycles*. Each school was assigned a performance target for each cycle based solely on its performance level during the first two years of that cycle. Schools that fell below their targets could be sanctioned, and schools that exceeded them by a sufficient amount received cash rewards. This system was a source of intense controversy within the state almost from its inception, but it has been viewed as a promising model by many reformers and observers of education throughout the nation.

KERA quickly produced large gains in scores on the KIRIS assessment. These gains were seen by many as signs that the reforms were improving educational performance; for example, the Kentucky Department of Education (KDE) entitled its press release of 1994 scores *"Celebrate the Progress!"* (Kentucky Department of Education, 1995a).

Assessment-based accountability, however, can lead to inflated gains. That is, scores can increase more than actual student learning warrants, creating an illusion of progress. This inflation can arise from numerous factors. For example, teachers may de-emphasize important material that is not likely to be tested in order to free up time for material emphasized on the test (e.g., Koretz, Barron, Mitchell, and Stecher, 1996). That is, they may focus on the content of the test itself rather than on the domain it is supposed to represent, thus raising scores more than they improve mastery of the domain. In extreme cases, teachers may focus on the content of specific test items. They may also narrow instruction relative to the intended domain by tailoring instruction narrowly to the rubrics used to score student work on the assessment (e.g., Stecher and Mitchell, 1995). And they may engage in inappropriate activities during testing sessions.

---

[1]The first such evaluation was an exception; it entailed a comparison of the first year alone to the average of the next two years.

In the case of systems using the more traditional, multiple-choice tests, the inflation of gains can be large, and the entire gain may even be illusory in some instances (Koretz, Linn, Dunbar, and Shepard, 1991). Indeed, some of the impetus for the "second wave" of education reform, in which educators are held accountable for scores on various performance assessments, was a growing recognition of the inflation of gains that can arise when traditional tests are used for accountability. There is no evidence, however, to indicate that forms of testing other than multiple choice are less susceptible to this problem.

Therefore, to evaluate the impact of the KERA program on student learning, it is essential to validate the observed gains in KIRIS scores—that is, to evaluate the extent to which these gains support the inference that student learning has indeed increased. This monograph reports the results of a study that used a variety of approaches to assess the validity of KIRIS gains from the first administration in 1992 through the 1995 and 1996 administrations.

SCOPE OF THE STUDY

While this study represents an unusually intensive effort to validate gains, it has major limitations.

Methods for validating gains are relatively primitive, and the data useful for this purpose in Kentucky—as in most states—are severely limited. Most traditional methods of validation do not take the possibility of inflated gains into account. Indeed, most of these methods are cross-sectional and therefore cannot address issues of change over time. Conventional methods for validating tests include examining the adequacy of an assessment's content, the behavior of individual items (e.g., tests of homogeneity and item bias), and convergent/discriminant evidence (the extent to which an assessment's correlations with other measures conform to expectations). All of these methods are typically applied cross-sectionally, and while they are essential for validating gains, they are insufficient for that purpose. For example, it will be shown below that scores on an accountability-oriented assessment and another assessment may maintain their correlation (a cross-sectional indication of validity) even while trends in mean scores on the two assessments show a huge and rapid divergence that calls the validity of gains into doubt. Relatively little attention has been given to developing methods directly germane to the validation of gains.

This report discusses cross-sectional evidence of validity only incidentally. Other efforts have been under way for years to obtain such evidence. For example, considerable evidence of this sort can be found in the KIRIS technical reports released periodically by KDE and in the report of an expert panel commissioned by the Office of Education Accountability (OEA) of the Kentucky General Assembly (Hambleton, et al., 1995). Although this evidence is mixed, it is not discussed here. Rather, we evaluate evidence directly pertinent to the validity of changes in scores.

Two broad types of evidence are discussed here: *internal* and *external*. Internal evidence derives from the KIRIS assessment itself. For example, one can look for clues about the validity of gains in performance differences on new test items versus items carried over from previous years. External evidence is based on comparisons of scores on KIRIS and other tests.

Only three sets of test scores suitable for comparison with KIRIS scores are available for much or all of Kentucky: scores from the National Assessment of Educational Progress (NAEP), from the American College Testing (ACT) college-admissions tests, and from two commercial achievement test batteries—the CTBS4 (Comprehensive Tests of Basic Skills) and CAT5 (California Achievement Tests)—currently used by many Kentucky districts. Of these three, the CTBS4 and CAT5 scores are not considered here for a variety of methodological reasons. (A comparison of trends on these tests and KIRIS can be found in Nitko, Stone, and Wang, 1997.) ACT scores are used, but ACT data are for a large but self-selected sample of high school students, and the overlap in content between the ACT and KIRIS tests is only moderate. NAEP scores provide the strongest evidence. The KIRIS assessment frameworks in reading and mathematics were expressly modeled after NAEP's, and NAEP occasionally tests representative samples at the state level. These samples, however, are obtained only infrequently. It was possible to compare NAEP and KIRIS for grade 4 reading from 1992 through only 1994 and for grade 4 and grade 8 mathematics from 1992 through 1996.

It is important to note that our analyses considered only the assessments from 1992 through 1995 and 1996. There were no aggregate gains on KIRIS in 1996, but our analysis of NAEP data necessarily included 1996 because NAEP was not administered in 1995.

A period of four years may seem long enough for evaluating an assessment program such as KIRIS, but it may not be. Experience has shown that scores often rise rapidly during the first few years of a testing program as familiarity with the test grows. A substantial share of these gains may not generalize to other tests and therefore may be seen as inflation of gains. Thus, one might find substantial inflation of gains over the first two to four years of an assessment and more meaningful gains thereafter. Moreover, KIRIS was evolving during the period covered by the analysis, and its effects in later years might have differed as a result. Nonetheless, the validity of KIRIS gains during the first four years is not a trivial concern—these gains have been widely presented as evidence of the program's success and have been used to allocate tens of millions of dollars in rewards to schools.

PLAN OF THE REPORT

Chapter 2 provides a very brief description of the KIRIS assessment and accountability system. The system is complex and has been documented in many other publications, so no effort is made to provide a detailed description here. It is necessary, however, to explain the basic characteristics of the system in order to make the evidence presented later in the report meaningful.

Chapter 3 provides a framework for validating gains on the KIRIS assessment—in particular, for evaluating external comparisons with other test data.

Chapter 4 describes trends in scores on KIRIS over the first four years of the program. Again, more detail is available in other reports. The purpose here is to describe the overall, statewide trends in performance, the validity of which is the focus of this report. To provide consistency over time and across the various types of analyses, the results reported here have all been calculated by RAND from Kentucky's assessment data and do not necessarily agree completely with those published by KDE. In most cases, any discrepancies are minor. A few, more substantial differences are noted in the text.

Chapter 5 summarizes evidence from past studies pertaining to the validity of score gains on KIRIS. Two documents are summarized: (1) the report of an expert panel (often called "the OEA Panel" or "the Hambleton Panel") convened by an agency of the Kentucky General Assembly to evaluate KIRIS after its first three years (Hambleton, et al., 1995); (2) a RAND series of surveys of Kentucky teachers and principals (Koretz, Barron, Mitchell, and Stecher, 1996).

Chapters 6 through 9 describe the results of our analyses. Chapter 6 discusses trends in the retention of students in grade. Chapters 7 and 8 discuss external evidence of the validity of gains, specifically, trends for NAEP and then for the ACT. In both cases, the findings of the OEA Panel (Hambleton, et al., 1995) are presented and then extended with additional analyses of newer data. Chapter 9 then presents a variety of internal evidence created from the KIRIS performance data themselves. It also details the several unconventional methods we used in our analyses.

Chapter 10 describes a number of the characteristics of KIRIS, such as changes in the design of the assessment over time, that might bear on the interpretation of the data presented in the earlier chapters.

Chapter 11 summarizes the empirical evidence, discusses its bearing on the validity of KIRIS score gains, and offers implications for both policy and further research.

The Appendix provides additional methodological detail pertaining to several aspects of the study: the creation of the KIRIS trend database we used; the methods used to standardize the KIRIS, NAEP, and ACT data; and the steps taken to create a merged file of ACT and KIRIS data.

2. DESCRIPTION OF KIRIS

Although the notion of holding schools accountable for students' performance on tests had gained considerable acceptance during the 1980s, KIRIS represented a major departure from previously common practice. The assessment was intended to be primarily performance based, and it has included a variety of constructed-response formats since its inception. The accountability system of which KIRIS is the cornerstone broke new ground in establishing sizable financial rewards and significant sanctions for schools on the basis of changes in their performance on an accountability index that primarily reflected scores on KIRIS but also included a variety of "noncognitive" indicators, such as dropout and attendance rates.

THE KIRIS ASSESSMENTS

The initial intent in establishing KIRIS was to implement a "primarily performance-based assessment . . . no later than the 1995-96 school year" (Kentucky Department of Education, 1993a, p. 2). No extant model of assessment was considered adequate, and KDE contracted with Advanced Systems for Measurement in Education to develop and implement the new program.[1] The assessment first put into place in the 1991-92 school year was seen as an interim program to be used while a more thoroughly performance-based program was developed.

This interim assessment initially had four components, although fewer than four were used to assess most subject areas. The so-called "transitional assessment" comprised two components, one using multiple-choice items and the other using open-ended paper-and-pencil items. The multiple-choice items were never used for accountability purposes. Both multiple-choice and open-response questions were matrix sampled. That is, the assessment was broken into multiple forms, each containing both common items (items that appeared in all forms) and matrix items (items that appeared in only one form). A given student received only one form and thus was administered only a portion of the total test in each subject area. In the case of open-response questions, each student received all of the common items in a subject area and a few (usually two) of the matrix items. Although common items formed the majority of any individual student's test booklet, they constituted only a modest share of the total assessment. Initially, there were three common open-response items per subject area in each grade (Kentucky Department of Education, 1993a). In both 1993 and 1994, each of the five core subject areas included five common open-response items and 24 matrix-sampled open-response items (Kentucky Department of Education, 1995b, p. 24). In 1996, there were from five to seven common open-response items (Kentucky Department of Education, 1997).

Common items are never reused and are made public. The more numerous matrix items can be reused and are supposed to be kept secure. In practice, some are reused, with or without alteration, while others are discarded. The number of new items introduced each

---

[1]Advanced Systems for Measurement in Education remained the prime contractor for the KIRIS assessment until 1997.

year has varied markedly. For example, in 1994, only seven of the items in the eighth-grade mathematics assessment were classified as new; in 1995, 15 were classified as new.[2] Teachers are free to use the released common items directly in instruction without modification or as more general guides to instruction. The use of matrix-sampled items in instruction, in contrast, is expressly forbidden.

The fact that much of the assessment is reused every year raises the risk of inflated gains. If teachers tailor their instruction too closely to the supposedly secure, reused matrix items, so that improved performance on those items does not generalize to other tasks from the same domain, then inferences about improvements in student performance will be exaggerated. Even if none of the items were reused, however, there would be considerable risk of inflation if the items were similar enough from year to year and sufficiently unrepresentative of the domain as a whole that teachers could effectively target them without targeting the entire domain from which they are sampled.

The third component of the assessment was performance events, complex performance tasks involving both group and individual work that were intended to take approximately one class period each. The final component was portfolio assessment, which was initially implemented only in writing (Kentucky Department of Education, 1993a). At the time of the program's inception, "the current vision [was] for an assessment system that is driven mainly by portfolios that are more broadly defined than those in use today" (Kentucky Department of Education, 1993a, p. 4).

Initially, testing was carried out in three grades: fourth, eighth, and twelfth. The transitional assessments and performance events were administered in mathematics, reading, science, and social studies. An on-demand direct test of writing was administered in addition to the writing portfolio assessment, but its results were not counted in the accountability index.

Based on their scores, students were each assigned to one of four performance levels, called Novice, Apprentice, Proficient, and Distinguished, in each subject area. These were considered discrete scores; that is, performance differences within a level were not recorded, and all students at any one of the levels were assigned the same numerical score. The numerical scores assigned to each performance level were assigned *a priori* as a matter of policy, not in response to patterns of performance on the test. These numerical values were 0 for Novice, 40 for Apprentice, 100 for Proficient, and 140 for Distinguished. Initially, the scores of individual students were not intended for reporting, because the matrix sampling of tasks makes individual scores error prone and noncomparable across testing forms, but the scores of students were averaged to provide a score for each school.

Since its inception, KIRIS has been modified substantially, although the changes have been quite different than the evolution towards portfolio assessment anticipated when the program was initiated. Portfolio assessment has been introduced in mathematics as well; it

---

[2]The items classified as new for technical purposes, however, included some that had been edited before reuse and therefore could not be treated as equivalent for the purpose of equating the assessment from one year to the next. The number of items that were qualitatively new was therefore smaller.

was added to the accountability index in cycle 2 but removed again in cycle 3. Multiple-choice items were dropped from the assessment entirely in 1995 because of the desire for performance-based assessments and assertions by KDE's assessment contractor that the assessment yielded sufficiently reliable scores without them. The OEA Panel criticized that decision and called for the reinstatement of multiple-choice testing to enhance "content validity, the reliability of school and student scores, score equating, and score reporting" (Hambleton, et al., 1995, p. 9), and KDE resumed using multiple-choice items as of 1997. Performance events were eliminated in 1996 because of difficulties equating the tasks across years. Most twelfth-grade testing was moved to the eleventh grade in 1995. Open-response testing was extended to two additional subject areas, arts and humanities and practical living/vocational studies.

The structure of the writing portfolio component remained stable over time, but its implementation was changed and strengthened. Teachers assign portfolio scores for their own students, and initial audits indicated that some teachers were assigning scores markedly higher than would be assigned by independent raters. The extent of this error in scores has declined sharply over time (Kentucky Department of Education, 1996a). This improvement in scoring presumably increased the validity of scores within any one year, but, ironically, it undermines the meaningfulness of trend estimates. That is, since trend estimates compare later scores (with less of this upward bias) to earlier scores (with more of it), improvements on the writing portfolios may be understated.

Our analyses were based on the open-response component of the transitional assessment, which received the greatest weight in the accountability index and was the only component used consistently over the period of the study. For that reason, the scores and trends we report may differ from those published by KDE, some of which reflect a larger number of assessment components. In most instances, the differences are minor. More substantial differences are noted in the text. Analysis is limited to four subjects: mathematics, reading, science, and social studies. Some analyses are further limited to one or two subjects or grades, to match the availability of external data and to make the scope of the analysis more manageable.

THE CURRICULAR BASIS FOR THE KIRIS ASSESSMENTS

The KIRIS assessments were not initially based on a specified curriculum, although their curricular basis has been gradually clarified and made more specific by KDE. The assessments were intended to reflect a set of performance standards, initially called the "valued outcomes" and later modified slightly and renamed the "academic expectations." These standards were supplemented in some instances by reference to the frameworks of NAEP. The valued outcomes and academic expectations were very general. For example, the 38 academic expectations for core academic concepts do not even mention numerous subject areas, such as algebra and chemistry. When subject areas are noted, no specificity is provided about the content to be covered. Examples include "students understand and appropriately use statistics and probability" and "students understand how living and nonliving things change over time and the factors that influence the changes" (see Figure 1).

TABLE 2-4
ACADEMIC EXPECTATIONS FOR GOAL 2: CORE ACADEMIC CONCEPTS

SCIENCE
1. Students understand scientific ways of thinking and working and use those methods to solve real-life problems.
2. Students identify, analyze, and use patterns such as cycles and trends to understand past and present events and predict possible future events.
3. Students identify and analyze systems and the ways their components work together or affect each other.
4. Students use the concept of scale and scientific models to explain the organization and functioning of living and nonliving things and predict other characteristics that might be observed.
5. Students understand that under certain conditions nature tends to remain the same or move toward a balance.
6. Students understand how living and nonliving things change over time and the factors that influence the changes.

MATHEMATICS
7. Students understand number concepts and use numbers appropriately and accurately.
8. Students understand various mathematical procedures and use them appropriately and accurately.
9. Students understand space and dimensionality concepts and use them appropriately and accurately.
10. Students understand measurement concepts and use measurements appropriately and accurately.
11. Students understand mathematical change concepts and use them appropriately and accurately.
12. Students understand mathematical structure concepts including the properties and logic of various mathematical systems.
13. Students understand and appropriately use statistics and probability.

SOCIAL STUDIES
14. Students understand the democratic principles of justice, equality, responsibility, and freedom and apply them to real-life situations.
15. Students can accurately describe various forms of government and analyze issues that relate to the rights and responsibilities of citizens in a democracy.
16. Students observe, analyze, and interpret human behaviors, social groupings, and institutions to better understand people and the relationships among individuals and among groups.
17. Students interact effectively and work cooperatively with the many ethnic and cultural groups of our nation and world.
18. Students understand economic principles and are able to make economic decisions that have consequences in daily living.
19. Students recognize and understand the relationship between people and geography and apply their knowledge in real-life situations.
20. Students understand, analyze, and interpret historical events, conditions, trends, and issues to develop historical perspective.
21. (Incorporated into 2.16)

ARTS AND HUMANITIES
22. Students create works of art and make presentations to convey a point of view.
23. Students analyze their own and others' artistic products and performances using accepted standards.
24. Students have knowledge of major works of art, music, and literature and appreciate creativity and the contributions of the arts and humanities.
25. In the products they make and the performances they present, students show that they understand how time, place, and society influence the arts and humanities such as languages, literature, and history.
26. Though the arts and humanities, students recognize that although people are different, they share some common experiences and attitudes.
27. Students recognize and understand the similarities and differences among languages.
28. Students understand and communicate in a second language.

PRACTICAL LIVING
29. Students demonstrate skills that promote individual well-being and healthy family relationships.
30. Students evaluate consumer products and services and make effective consumer decisions.
31. Students demonstrate the knowledge and skills they need to remain physically healthy and to accept responsibility for their own physical well-being.
32. Students demonstrate strategies for becoming and remaining mentally and emotionally healthy.
33. Students demonstrate the skills to evaluate and use services and resources available in their community.
34. Students perform physical movement skills effectively in a variety of settings.
35. Students demonstrate knowledge and skills that promote physical activity and involvement in physical activity throughout their lives.

VOCATIONAL STUDIES
36. Students use strategies for choosing and preparing for a career.
37. Students demonstrate skills and work habits that lead to success in future schooling and work.
38. Students demonstrate skills such as interviewing, writing resumes, and completing applications that are needed to be accepted into college or other postsecondary training or to get a job.

SOURCE: Kentucky Department of Education, 1995b, p. 8.

Figure 1—Academic Expectations for Core Academic Concepts

Work on a more detailed description of the KIRIS domains began early in the program's existence, and in June 1993—after the second of the four administrations of KIRIS considered here—KDE published *Transformations: Kentucky's Curriculum Framework* (Kentucky Department of Education, 1993b). A summer 1992 draft of *Transformations* and the June 1993 publication were sent to schools and school districts. In September 1995, after the fourth administration of KIRIS, KDE published a revision of the *Transformations* that reflected the replacement of the "valued outcomes" by the slightly modified "academic expectations." The revised version was placed on a KDE Web site and was also sold by KDE (Durbin, 1998).

The *Transformations* document elaborated considerably on the academic expectations but was still quite general. For example, the explanation of academic expectation 2.10, "students understand measurement concepts and use measurements appropriately and accurately" includes "demonstrators" that make this expectation more concrete (Figure 2). Some are general ("apply trigonometry to real world problems"), while others are more specific ("determine the area of irregular shapes by subdivision using manipulatives"). There are very few demonstrators, however, for each expectation. In the case of expectation 2.10, there are five for elementary school, three for middle school, and four for high school. These are accompanied by four or five sample activities each for elementary, middle, and high schools, as well as half a dozen examples of applications of these concepts in curricular areas other than mathematics. A similar level of detail is provided for academic expectation 2.11, "students understand mathematical change concepts and use them appropriately and accurately," which appears to be the academic expectation that subsumes most of algebra. For example, one of the three middle school demonstrators is "represent patterns in several ways (e.g., graphs, ordered pairs, verbal statements, algebraic rules)" (Figure 3). The most specific of the six high school demonstrators is "investigate the properties of various types of functions (e.g., linear, quadratic, logarithmic, trigonometric, etc.)."

In 1996, after the last of the KIRIS assessments considered here, KDE published and distributed to schools a set of more-detailed guidelines for most content areas called *Core Content for Assessment* (Kentucky Department of Education, 1996c). The guide covering core content for mathematics assessment, for example, was "designed to clarify and further define/refine the mathematics content outlined in *Kentucky's Learning Goals and Academic Expectations* and in *Transformations: Kentucky's Curriculum Framework*" (Kentucky Department of Education, 1996c). The high school specifications from *Core Content* for geometry/measurement are shown in Figure 4, and the specifications for algebraic ideas (not a separate academic expectation) are shown in Figure 5 (Note that the content is cumulative across grades, so high school students, teachers, and parents are told to attend to the elementary and middle school content as well.) The *Core Content* guides are substantially more detailed and specific than the earlier curriculum documents, and they note a number of specific content elements, such as English and metric measurement systems, the concepts of slope and rate, the basic trigonometric measures, and linear, quadratic, and exponential equations and functions.

Thus, for the first four administrations of KIRIS—until the publication of *Core Content*—the frameworks provided by KDE offered teachers little concrete guidance about the specific content and skills students would need to do well on the KIRIS assessments. Over the last few years, educators have been offered somewhat more clarity about the curricular expectations underlying KIRIS, but the level of detail is still far less than one would have with a curriculum-based examination system such as the College Board

Goal 2: Apply Core Concepts and Principles

Academic Expectation

2.10: Students understand measurement concepts and use measurement appropriately and accurately.

Learning Links: Biorhythms / Circular Motion / Sound Waves / Scale Drawing / Light / Recipes / Sewing / Electricity / Drafting / Unit Pricing / Construction / Sports / Meteorology / Latitude and Longitude / Seismograph

Related Concepts: Maximum/Minimum / Trigonometry / Perimeter / Nonstandard Units / Area / Mass / Time / Metric/ Customary Units / Volume / Angle / Money / Vectors / Dimensions / Weight / Rate / Temperature / Area Bounded by a Curve

Elementary Demonstrators

Middle School Demonstrators

High School Demonstrators

Demonstrators should be read from bottom to top, but need not be demonstrated sequentially.

Elementary	Middle School	High School
• Make estimates and measurements in solving problems using appropriate tools and units. • Use nonstandard and standard units of measure. • Develop concepts of length, capacity, weight, mass, area, perimeter, volume, time, temperature, angle, circumference, and money through use of manipulatives. • Compare and order mass, length, area, and volume. • Conserve mass, length, area, and volume.	• Develop, through investigation, the formulas for perimeter, area, and volume. • Determine the area of irregular shapes by subdivision using manipulatives. • Extend the concepts of length, area, volume, mass, weight, capacity, time, angle, perimeter, money, circumference, and temperature using measurement tools and models.	• Investigate the concepts of rates, energy, and other derived and indirect measurements. • Explore periodic real world phenomena. • Apply trigonometry to real world problems. • Determine surface areas and volumes of solids in solving nonroutine real world problems.

Sample Teaching/Assessment Strategies: _____

Collaborative Process: Cooperative Learning, Peer Tutoring • **Community-Based Instruction:** Field Studies, Mentoring, Service Learning • **Problem Solving:** Brainstorming, Inquiry, Formulating Models, Future Problem Solving, Research • **Technology/Tools:** Manipulatives, Computers, Video Production

These sample strategies offer ideas and are not meant to limit teacher resourcefulness. More strategies are found in the resource section.

Ideas for Incorporating Community Resources: _____

• Interview building contractors to explain measurement as it applies to construction and cost.

• Observe and record the ways measurement is used by employees during a visit to a medical laboratory (e.g., T-waves on an EKG, or number of blood cells on a blood smear).

• Visit an amusement park to investigate application of laws of physics on various rides.

SOURCE: Kentucky Department of Education, 1995c, p. 88.

Figure 2—Demonstrators for Understanding and Use of Measurement Concepts

Goal 2: Apply Core Concepts and Principles

Academic Expectation

2.11: Students understand mathematical change concepts and use them appropriately and accurately.

Learning Links: Nature / Evolution / Chaos / Topology / Human Development / Mutations / Chemical Reactions / Geopolitical / Fractals / Rock Formations / Migration

Related Concepts: Transformations / Trigonometric Functions / Continuous vs. Discrete / Algebraic Representations/ Variables / Limit / Sequences / Functions / Matrix Representations / Series / Patterns

Elementary Demonstrators   *Middle School Demonstrators*   *High School Demonstrators*

Demonstrators should be read from bottom to top, but need not be demonstrated sequentially.

Elementary	Middle School	High School
• Use variables, represented by manipulatives, to express relationships involving change. • Explore the concepts of unknown quantities and effects of change (functions). • Extend and create patterns and generalize structures from patterns (e.g., square numbers, geometric patterns, patterns in nature) in number sequences. • Observe patterns of change (e.g., seasons, height, weather) in everyday life and discuss causes and effects.	• Explore functions that can be derived from physical models, data, and other mathematical representations. • Investigate patterns in number sequences and relate to real world experiences. • Represent patterns in several ways (e.g., graphs, ordered pairs, verbal statements, algebraic rules).	• Investigate the properties of various types of functions, (e.g., linear, quadratic, logarithmic, trigonometric, etc.). • Determine appropriate model to represent change in data (i.e., discrete or continuous). • Use curve fitting to predict change. • Explain how a change in one quantity affects a change in another. • Model a variety of problem situations with similar functions. • Analyze the effects of parametric changes on graphs.

Sample Teaching/Assessment Strategies: _____

Collaborative Process: Cooperative Learning • **Community-Based Instruction:** Mentoring • **Continuous Progress Assessment:** Observation, Performance Events, Portfolio Development • **Graphic Organizers:** Graphic Representations, Flowchart • **Problem Solving:** Inquiry, Questioning, Case Studies, Creative Problem Solving, Future Problem Solving, Formulating Models, Simulations • **Technology/Tools:** Manipulatives, Computers, Multimedia

These sample strategies offer ideas and are not meant to limit teacher resourcefulness. More strategies are found in the resource section.

Ideas for Incorporating Community Resources: _____

• Contact public agencies for data specific to the community (e.g., water company for information on water pressure and flow rate, U.S. Census Bureau for demographic data).

• Take a field trip to the local automobile dealership and have a salesperson explain how the NADA (Blue Book) standards are used to determine the price of used cars.

• Survey businesses to discover how future sales/services are projected from current sales figures and how that affects future staffing.

SOURCE: Kentucky Department of Education, 1995c, p. 92.

Figure 3—Demonstrators for Understanding and Use of Mathematical Change Concepts

---

Students should understand:

Algebraic transformations

Transformations in geometric systems

Spatial relationships such as betweenness, perpendicularity, and parallelism

The structure of standard measurement systems (English, metric)

Ratio measures such as slope and rate

Trigonometric measures (sine, cosine, tangent, degrees)

Students should be able to:

Use transformations on figures and numbers

Describe elements which change and elements which do not change under transformations

Construct geometric figures using a variety of techniques (e.g., straightedge and compass, paper folding, three-dimensional models, MIRA)

Use methods of indirect measurement (e.g., shadow method or mirror method for finding the height of a tree)

Use Pythagorean Theorem

Students should understand the following relationships:

How properties of geometric shapes relate to each other

How trigonometric ratios relate to right triangles

How algebraic procedures and geometric concepts are related

How position in the plane can be represented using rectangular coordinates

---

Figure 4—High School Core Content in Geometry/Measurement

Students should understand:

Variables and constants in expressions, equations, and inequalities

Systems of equations and their representations

Linear, quadratic, and exponential equations and functions

Students should be able to:

Solve and graph a variety of equations and inequalities

Construct tables of numeric values of equations and inequalities

Identify the characteristics of the graphs of functions: domain, intercepts, etc.

Represent patterns using functions

Students should understand the following relationships:

How formulas, tables, graphs, words, and equations of functions relate to each other

How different parameters affect graphs of functions (e.g., compare the graph of $y = 3x2$ to the graph $y = x2$)

Figure 5—High School Core Content in Algebraic Ideas

Advanced Placement tests or the traditional New York State Regents examinations. For example, *Core Content* explains that students should "understand . . . linear, quadratic, and exponential equations and functions." But how much mastery is needed? In many curricula for college-bound students, that single sentence would point to many weeks of study across two years of algebra. Even one single element of that sentence, quadratic equations, can map to weeks of study in a second-year algebra course, including factoring quadratic equations using both the quadratic equation and the method of complete squares, evaluating discriminants as a means of determining the number and type of roots, evaluating the vertex and determining whether it is a minimum or a maximum, and finding the solutions to systems of quadratic equalities and inequalities. It may also include application of these methods to real-world problems, such as finding the maximum area of the rectangular plot enclosed by a fixed length of fencing.

A mathematics teacher concerned about performance on an assessment must decide how much of this material is worth the considerable time it requires, given that the total amount of available instructional time is essentially fixed. Even the most detailed of the curricular guidance offered by KDE, the *Core Content*, does not answer this question. Faced with this uncertainty, teachers may turn to previous versions of the assessment for concrete guidance about what is meant by "understand[ing] . . . linear, quadratic, and exponential equations and functions." If they were to look at the assessments their students take, they would find that the answers may vary. As explained below, KIRIS and the ACT, for example, suggest different levels of mastery of this content. This issue of curricular specificity (or the lack of specificity), which arises in many other assessment-based accountability systems as well, is revisited in Chapter 11 because it may have important implications for the validity of score gains.

THE KIRIS ACCOUNTABILITY SYSTEM

Scores on the KIRIS assessments are combined with a number of noncognitive indicators to create a single accountability index. The construction of this index has been modified a few times but has not been fundamentally changed. The description here is of the initial index (see Kentucky Department of Education, 1994).

The "cognitive index"—the assessment-based portion of the total accountability index—was initially created from scores in reading, mathematics, science, social studies, and writing. The reading portion of the cognitive index reflected only the percentages of a school's students at each of the performance levels on the transitional assessment. In mathematics, science, and social studies, these percentages from the transitional assessment were combined with the percentages at each of the levels on the performance events, with the transitional assessment given four times the weight given to the performance events. In writing, the only data used were the percentages of students at each performance level on the portfolio assessment.

While the score of any individual student can take only one of four values in each subject (0 for Novice, 40 for Apprentice, 100 for Proficient, or 140 for Distinguished), a school's cognitive index in each subject is obtained by averaging the scores of all students and is therefore a continuous variable that in theory can range from 0 (all students at the Novice level) to 140 (all students at the Distinguished level). Initial scores on the cognitive index were typically low. In 1992, the mean score on the cognitive index was 21 in grade 4, 25 in grade 8, and 29 in grade 12 (Kentucky Department of Education, 1995b, Table 11-3).

The noncognitive indicators were initially attendance rate, retention rate (retention in grade), dropout rate, and "successful transition rate." KDE defines this last indicator as "the ratio of the number of 'successful' high school graduates to graduate membership" and states that " 'successful transition to adult life' is identified by such criteria as full-time enrollment in post-secondary school, employment in a non-temporary position at least 30 hours per week, active military status, or a combination of these situations totaling at least 30 hours per week" (Kentucky Department of Education, 1994, p. 4-7). Scores on the noncognitive index can in theory range from 0 to 100. Initial scores were high and did not vary greatly among schools. In 1992, the average score on the noncognitive index was 96 in grade 4, 97 in grade 8, and 93 in grade 12 (Kentucky Department of Education, 1995b, Table 11-3). Thus, there was little room for improvement.

The total accountability index was created by averaging the noncognitive index and the five components of the cognitive index. This average was unweighted, so each of the components—for example, the noncognitive index or science performance—constituted one-sixth of each school's score on the accountability index.

The system for assigning rewards and sanctions is based on the expectation that regardless of its starting point, each school will reach an index of 100, corresponding to having every student at the Proficient level, in 20 years. The implementation of this simple concept, however, is complex. Progress toward this goal is measured at two-year intervals, called *bienniums* or *accountability cycles*. Each biennium, schools are assigned a target, called a *threshold,* based on their expected rate of progress. Rewards or sanctions are assigned at the end of each cycle based on two factors: (1) the margin by which schools exceed or fall below their thresholds for that biennium, and (2) the percentage of students remaining at the Novice level. To receive rewards, schools have to exceed their improvement goal by more than one point and move 10 percent of their Novice students to a higher level (Kentucky Department of Education, 1995a, p. 8). With the exception of the first cycle, progress during each cycle is measured by comparing a two-year average to the previous two-year average to lessen the impact of annual fluctuations in scores. Thus, the average of scores from each two-year period serves as both the target during one cycle and the baseline during the next cycle.

Although the improvement targets for schools are nominally clear in this system, they were in important respects unknown and arbitrary when the system was initiated. For example, the system deliberately requires lower-performing schools to achieve nominally larger improvements—that is, larger increases on the accountability index. The system was established, however, before the assessment had ever been administered. At that time, no one knew what the distribution of performance would be—for example, the average scores and the range and variability of scores across both students and schools. Without that information, there was no way to know how large the improvement targets for any schools were relative to some standard, such as the variability of student performance or research evidence on the plausible size of average gains. The requirements for score gains required by this system are estimated below, in Chapter 4.

3. A FRAMEWORK FOR EVALUATING THE VALIDITY OF SCORE GAINS

The validity of gains on KIRIS (or any other assessment) depends on the inferences that people base on those gains. For example, say that scores on a state's eighth-grade mathematics assessment increased sharply while the state's scores on the NAEP mathematics assessment did not increase. Whether this constitutes negative news about validity depends in part on how users interpret the scores. If users construe scores on the state test to indicate mastery of a domain of mathematics that overlaps considerably with that measured by NAEP, this divergence of trends would indeed be negative news. But if users understand scores on the state test to indicate mastery of a domain of mathematics that overlaps little with the domain of NAEP, then the divergence of trends would not be reason for concern.

However, validity hinges on more than the intended inference or domain of generalization. Under some circumstances, gains on an assessment may not provide reasonable evidence of increased mastery even of the assessment's own intended domain of generalization. That is, score gains can be inflated, creating an overestimate of meaningful improvements in students' mastery of the domain that the assessment is intended to measure (e.g., Koretz, Linn, Dunbar, and Shepard, 1991).

To help interpret score gains, it is helpful to consider (1) the possible components of score gains, and (2) potential sources of these different components. We illustrate these issues here by making a comparison between KIRIS and NAEP. This is a particularly important comparison because NAEP represents a degree of national consensus about performance goals and because KIRIS was intended to measure a domain reasonably similar to that of NAEP in mathematics and reading.

Increases in scores on both KIRIS and NAEP can be broken down into several components. In Figure 6, total KIRIS gains are shown as a shaded rectangle broken into three parts. The first, labeled A (the area to the left of the dashed line), is inflation—that is, score increases that do not indicate gains in mastery of the domains of knowledge and skills that KIRIS is intended to measure. The remaining gains on KIRIS (to the right of the dashed line) do represent meaningful increases in mastery of the KIRIS domains, but these gains are broken into two parts. The first part, labeled B, represents nongeneralizable real gains on KIRIS—in this case, improvements in mastery of parts of the KIRIS domains that are not measured by NAEP and that therefore do not cause NAEP scores to rise. The final component of KIRIS gains, labeled C, is score increases that represent improved mastery of parts of the domains that are shared by KIRIS and NAEP. These would cause NAEP scores to rise as well and are therefore labeled "generalizable" real gains. (The relative size of these three components in the figure is arbitrary.) Of course, if KIRIS were compared to a test other than NAEP, the breakdown between generalizable and nongeneralizable real gains would likely be different.

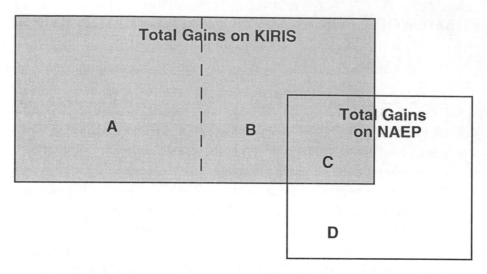

Note: Drawing is not to scale.

Shaded area, A ∪ B ∪ C: Total Gain on KIRIS

C ∪ D: Total Gains on NAEP

A: KIRIS Gains Attributable to Inflation

B (does not include C): Nongeneralizable Real Gains on KIRIS

C: Generalizable Real Gains on both KIRIS and NAEP

D: Nongeneralizable Real Gains on NAEP

Figure 6—Decomposition of KIRIS Gains

Note that NAEP gains are shown in Figure 6 as consisting of two parts. In addition to the generalizable real gains (labeled C), there are also nongeneralizable real gains, labeled D. Just as differences between NAEP and KIRIS make possible meaningful gains on KIRIS that are not reflected in NAEP, they also make possible meaningful gains on NAEP that are not reflected in KIRIS. Because there is no reason to expect inflation of NAEP gains—teachers are not generally under pressure to raise scores on the assessment and typically know little if anything about its content—NAEP gains are shown in Figure 6 as comprising only two parts, not three. However, if teachers are given incentives to raise NAEP scores, either directly or by being held accountable for performance on a test very tightly modeled after NAEP, one might see inflation of NAEP gains as well.

Inflation of gains can arise for a wide variety of reasons. The term *inflated gains* is used here solely to indicate observed gains in scores that are larger than actual improvements in student proficiency, which can result in score gains that do not generalize to other measures. Inflation can arise from misleadingly low scores at the onset of a trend, misleadingly high scores at the end of a trend, or both. The presence of inflated gains need not indicate inappropriate practices, although in many cases inappropriate practices do contribute to it. Scores will often rise on a new assessment over the first several years of its use as students and teachers become more familiar with the assessment, and some of these gains from familiarization may constitute inflation of gains. For example, if a test is sufficiently novel, initial scores may be misleadingly low because of students' uncertainty about the required performance. This might happen, for example, if a novel format confused students. Over time, even if student mastery of the domain does not increase, this initial negative bias is likely to abate, causing an increase in scores that does not indicate real gains in student proficiency. Familarization can also alter teachers' behaviors in ways that raise scores. As teachers become more familiar with the new assessment, they are likely to focus their instruction increasingly on the knowledge and skills it emphasizes. This change can be desirable and can lead to real gains in student proficiency, but it can also lead to inflation— for example, if teachers focus too narrowly on the particular types of tasks used in the assessment, or if they focus too narrowly on the content included in the assessment at the cost of neglecting other important aspects of the intended domain. Inflation can also arise from changes in student motivation. If successive cohorts of students become increasingly motivated to do well on an assessment, gains in scores would to some degree reflect increased effort in the test-taking situation rather than increased mastery of the domain—even if the later scores produced by more-motivated students were more accurate than the earlier scores of less-motivated students. Inflation of scores can also arise from inappropriate test preparation or administration, or it can stem from changes in tested cohorts, such as increases in retention in grade or increased exclusion of low-scoring students from testing.

The validity of KIRIS gains depends on both the inferences users draw and the relative sizes of the score-gain components illustrated in Figure 6, above. In most cases, the portion of total score gains labeled "C: generalizable real gains on both KIRIS and NAEP" would be considered a meaningful improvement in proficiency. The extent to which the portion labeled "B: nongeneralizable real gains on KIRIS" is considered meaningful, however, depends on the domains about which users draw conclusions. The gains in area B reflect skills and knowledge not represented to any appreciable degree in NAEP. Users may place greater or lesser value on this more idiosyncratic set of knowledge and skills. At the extreme, some users may consider all of this content important, even if there were no gains shared with NAEP (that is, if area C were essentially empty). Thus, an upper-bound estimate of valid gains would be the sum of B and C—that is, the portion of total observed gains (A plus B plus C) that does not represent just inflation. For inferences that focus on content and skills that are not idiosyncratic, valid gains would be represented by the smaller area, C. For many of the likely inferences, valid gains would fall somewhere between these two extremes.

The simple discrepancy between gains on the two assessments—that is, the difference between total gains on KIRIS (A $\cup$ B $\cup$ C) and total gains on NAEP (C $\cup$ D)—is therefore an adequate measure of inflated scores only if users base similar inferences on both tests. The more users draw inferences about scores on the two tests that focus on different skills or knowledge, the larger the meaningful but nongeneralizable gains (area B for KIRIS and area

D for NAEP) will be. If area B is larger than area D, meaningful gains on KIRIS may be larger than total gains on NAEP, but if area B is smaller than area D, meaningful gains on KIRIS may be *smaller* than total gains on NAEP.

4. TRENDS IN KIRIS SCORES

Any effort to validate observed gains in scores must begin with a description of them. The descriptions generally published in Kentucky, however, are difficult to understand. The four-category KIRIS scale is not necessarily comparable across subjects or grade levels. That is, students may find it more difficult to reach a given level in one subject or grade than in another. In addition, the relationships of the KIRIS scale to reporting metrics used in other places are obscure.

We standardized KIRIS scores to make trends comparable across subjects and grades and to trends observed in other assessment results. We begin here by describing how we standardized KIRIS scores. We then use the standardized scores to illustrate the magnitude of the changes required by the KIRIS accountability section. This is followed by a description of KIRIS trends from 1992 through 1996, the longest time period used in any of the validity analyses below, based on RAND's reanalysis of KIRIS data. Results of the 1997 assessment were released in December 1997, as this report was being completed, and RAND had not yet received a copy of the 1997 data files when this was written. Accordingly, only a brief description of the 1997 results, based on KDE tabulations that are not entirely consistent with those used here, is presented.

PLACING KIRIS ON A COMMON SCALE

KIRIS trends are reported on a four-point ordinal scale (often called the *NAPD scale,* for the Novice, Apprentice, Proficient, and Distinguished performance levels), the points on which are assigned values of 0, 40, 100, and 140. For several reasons, this scale makes interpretation difficult.

First, the scale understates or ignores some changes and overstates others. For example, as Catterall, et al. (1998) pointed out, this scale is insensitive to performance changes within any one level (e.g., Apprentice). It also treats all changes that cross the divide between a given level and the next as equivalent, even if they differ in size. For example, moving from low in the Apprentice range to high in the Proficient range counts the same as moving from high Apprentice to low Proficient.

Second, both the selection of cut-points and the assignment of numerical values to them are arbitrary, and the choice of a different arbitrary scale could alter trends in scores. A scale with different cut-points might register either less or more change. In addition, simply assigning different numerical values to the cut-points would alter some measures of change.[1]

---

[1]Catterall, et al. (1998) show that the *percentage increase* in the index is particularly sensitive to changes in the arbitrary values assigned to the performance levels. In one example, they show that using values of 1, 2, 3, and 4 for student scores, rather than the current values of 0, 40, 100, and 140, would reduce the apparent 1997 percentage increase in eleventh-grade reading by more than half.

Third, even though the scale appears similar in all subjects, it may not be. There is no guarantee, for example, that a change from Apprentice to Proficient in reading is comparable to the nominally similar increase in science. Finally, because the KIRIS scale is unique, KIRIS results cannot be compared directly to results from other assessments without some type of transformation.

The best way to address these problems would be to analyze trends using a different scale—specifically, the continuous, approximately normal theta scale that was produced by the KIRIS scaling starting in 1993 but never used for reporting. Theta estimates were not produced for 1992, however, and we needed 1992 scores, for example, for comparison to NAEP scores.

As an alternative, we standardized the KIRIS NAPD scores separately by grade and subject so that trends could be expressed in standard deviation units. This approach makes trends comparable in an important sense from one subject to another and reduces the impact of the arbitrary choice of scale on trend estimates. We standardized trends in each subject area in terms of the standard deviation of student scores in that subject in 1994. For this purpose, scores were assigned the values of 0, 40, 100, and 140 used by KDE.

Because KIRIS scores are on a discrete scale with arbitrary values, however, standardizing them is inherently ambiguous. Moreover, in the first year of the program (1992), scores were highly concentrated at the Novice level. This makes standardization less appropriate and also leads to an unusually small standard deviation, which in turn exaggerates the size of trends in standardized scores. To address the problem of concentrated scores, we used data from the midpoint of the period considered here (1994), when scores were markedly less concentrated, as the basis for standardization.[2] We tested the adequacy of this standardization by comparing selected results to those obtained with the theta scale available beginning in 1993. This comparison suggests that standardized NAPD scores provide a reasonable if conservative approximation—that is, they may modestly understate the size of KIRIS trends (see Appendix).

THE MAGNITUDE OF CHANGE REQUIRED BY KIRIS

The size and rapidity of the score increases required by an accountability system may powerfully influence teachers' responses to it and thus may affect the validity of score gains. While too modest a requirement may provide an insufficient incentive to change instruction, too large a requirement may increase the risk of inflated score gains. The larger the requirement for score increases, the greater the incentive to focus instruction specifically on the assessment, even at the cost of reduced emphasis on other important aspects of the curriculum and the intended domain of generalization. In addition, rates of improvement that are considerably greater than those observed in other large-scale interventions would be reason to question the meaning of score gains.

---

[2]In presenting standardized trend estimates, we set the mean for the first administration, in 1992, equal to zero, even though we used 1994 standard deviations, so that all values could be interpreted as changes from the start of the testing program.

On the scale used for the accountability index, lower-performing schools were required to make larger and more rapid gains. For example, the average school with a fourth grade in 1992 had a total accountability index of 33.6 (Kentucky Department of Education, 1995b, Table 11-3). That school would have to increase its index by 66.4 points over 20 years to meet its expectation—that is, to reach its threshold. A school with an initial score of 20, roughly at the bottom of the initial distribution, would have to raise its index by 80 points, while a school starting at a score of 45, near the top of the initial distribution, would need to increase its score by 55 points, roughly two-thirds as much. Because the noncognitive components of the index counted relatively little, varied relatively little, and had only modest room for improvement, nearly all of these increases had to be accomplished by raising scores on the assessment.

The KIRIS scale is arbitrary, however, and while these required improvements appear large, their actual size can only be judged by transforming them into another metric that is better understood. The standardized scores used here show the required gains as fractions or multiples of a standard deviation. This approach could clarify how large the required gains are relative to both the current distribution of student performance and past experience with large-scale educational interventions. Unfortunately, given the characteristics of the KIRIS scale, this cannot be done precisely. The ambiguities in standardizing KIRIS scores noted earlier are more serious when considering the very large increases required over 20 years than when examining changes in performance over a few years.

Nonetheless, it is possible to get a rough estimate of the required improvements, and they appear to be very large. Two different approaches to standardization suggest that meeting the required thresholds would require gains in many cases of approximately two standard deviations or more over 20 years, and possibly three standard deviations in some extreme cases. Thus, in each two-year accountability cycle, schools would need to raise scores roughly 0.2 standard deviation or more. To obtain rewards would require somewhat more improvement, increasing the total required gain by roughly an additional 10 to 20 percent each biennium.

These expected rates of change are by any standard very large—indeed, unprecedented in large-scale educational interventions. Translating the expected changes into percentiles provides one indication of their magnitude. A mean increase of 2 standard deviations on a continuous, normally distributed distribution would mean that fully half of all students in the year 2012 would have to exceed a level of performance exceeded by only two out of 100 students in 1992. An increase of 2.5 standard deviations would place the median student at a level reached by only six students in 1,000 in 1992. The required change would also be considerably larger than some of the larger current group differences in achievement. For example, the mean difference in eighth-grade mathematics in the Third International Mathematics and Science Study (TIMSS) between Japan (one of the highest-scoring countries) and the U.S. (which ranked 18th of the 25 nations with good samples) was about 1.1 standard deviations (Beaton, et al., 1996).[3] The mean difference in grade 8 mathematics between non-Hispanic whites and African Americans was about 0.9 standard deviation in the 1990 NAEP and about 0.8 standard deviation in the 1988 base-year cohort of the National Educational Longitudinal Study (Berends and Koretz, 1996).

A final standard of comparison is the nationwide decline in test scores during the 1960s and 1970s. This decline, which appears to reflect the combined influences of educational practices and broader societal changes (Koretz, 1987), provided a substantial share of the impetus for the education reform movements of the 1980s and 1990s. During the entire period of the decline, the average scores on most tests dropped by less than 0.4 standard deviation, and the drop on some tests was considerably smaller (Koretz, 1986).[4] In other words, the gain that the average Kentucky school was expected to show over 20 years was five times or more the size of the total achievement decline.

STATEWIDE TRENDS IN MEAN KIRIS SCORES

In many instances, gains on the KIRIS assessment have been very large, but there have been important exceptions. KDE has published scores on the KIRIS cognitive index for each tested subject area in each year of the assessment. Currently, the cognitive index excludes the performance events, which have proven problematic and have not been used in every year. The writing index scores reflect the writing portfolios. The cognitive index is presented on a scale of 0 to 140, where Novice students are counted as 0, Apprentice students are given a score of 40, Proficient students are counted as 100, and Distinguished students are scored as 140. Thus, a statewide mean of 100 would be obtained if all students were at the Proficient level.

Statewide means on this index increased substantially but inconsistently from 1992 through 1995. In some instances, the increases were dramatic. From 1995 to 1996, however, there was little improvement in any subject or grade, and scores declined appreciably in some instances.

In the fourth grade, the largest and most consistent gain through 1995 was in reading (Figure 7).[5] In the first three years of the program, the average reading score on the NAPD scale increased from 20 to 55; in the fourth year, it rose about another point. Mathematics scores started lower and improved less from the first to the second year of the program, but the increase over the four-year period was nonetheless very large, from a mean of 16 to one of 39 on the index. (As noted earlier, these results reflect the open-response component of the transitional assessment. Some mathematics trend results published by KDE include

---

[3]Mathematics performance is more variable in Japan than in the U.S. The mean difference between Japan and the U.S. is equal to 1.0 times the Japanese standard deviation and 1.2 times the U.S. standard deviation. These calculations are based on Table 1.1, Figure 1.1, and Table E.1 in Beaton, et al., 1996.

[4]The SAT Verbal scale and the ACT social studies and mathematics tests showed declines of more than 0.40 standard deviation, but these trends were exacerbated by changes in the selectivity of the groups taking the tests.

[5]The 1992 means used here differ from those in earlier reports published by KDE, which used an older scale. Ours were obtained by subtracting from 1993 means on the current scale the change from 1992 to 1993 on the older scale.

portfolio scores and therefore differ appreciably from these.) Both social studies and science showed smaller gains that began later.

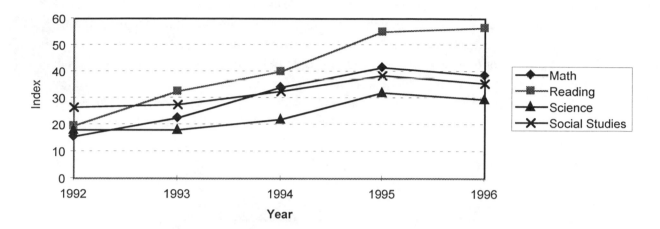

Figure 7—Mean KIRIS Scores by Subject, Grade 4

The standardized increase in reading scores over the four-year period was 1.4 standard deviations, and the increase over the first three years was 1.3 standard deviations (Figure 8). The standardized increases in mathematics and science were smaller—0.6 and 0.5 standard deviation, respectively, over the four-year period, even adding in the small declines in 1996. These still represent very large gains, however, particularly for such a short period. The gain in social studies was roughly 0.3 standard deviation, still a sizable increase by most standards.

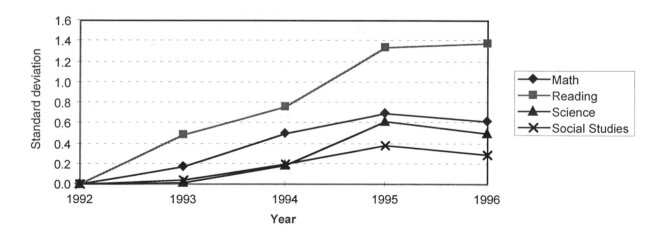

Figure 8—Cumulative Change in KIRIS Scores by Subject, Grade 4, in Standard Deviations

The observed gains in eighth grade were smaller than those in fourth grade in every subject but social studies, but they were substantial nonetheless. Measured in terms of the KIRIS accountability index, the gains from 1992 to 1995 were 26 points in mathematics, 11 points in reading and social studies, and 9 points in science (Figure 9). The gain in mathematics during the first three years corresponded to about 0.6 standard deviation (Figure 10), only slightly smaller than the gain in fourth-grade mathematics. In reading, the gains in eighth grade were much smaller than those in fourth grade, and they persisted only two years—from 1992 to 1994. They were nonetheless considerable, totaling 0.36 standard deviation even with the slight decline from 1994 to 1995 (Figure 10). Gains in science and social studies were sizable over the first three years—0.4 and 0.3 standard deviation, respectively—but were largely offset by declines in the fourth year, leaving total increases of 0.15 and 0.10 standard deviation, respectively.

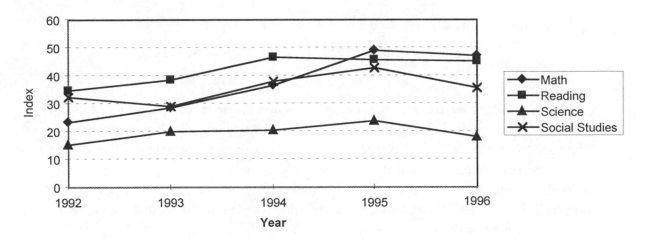

Figure 9—Mean KIRIS Scores by Subject, Grade 8

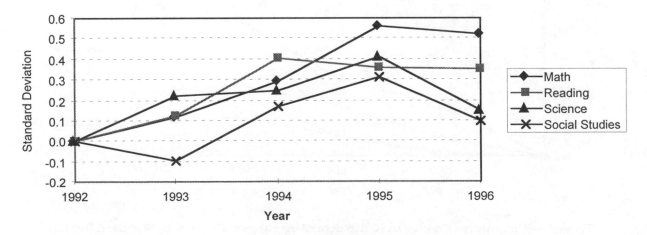

Figure 10—Cumulative Change in KIRIS Scores by Subject, Grade 8, in Standard Deviations

Trends in the scores of high school students are complicated by a change in KIRIS. Through 1994, KIRIS was administered to students in the twelfth grade, but starting in 1995, it was administered to students in the eleventh grade. To show trends, we adjusted the scores of eleventh-grade students to place them on the same scale as those of the twelfth-grade students tested earlier. (Our method is described in the Appendix.)

Over the four-year period from 1992 to 1996, gains in grade 11/12 ranged from 35 points in social studies to 46 points in mathematics (Figure 11). When standardized (Figure 12), these score increases were similar to those in grade 8 in mathematics (0.5 standard deviation), reading (0.3 standard deviation), and social studies (0.1 standard deviation). The increase was larger in science, about 0.4 standard deviation, in comparison to 0.15 in grade 8. The pattern over time, however, was less stable in grade 11/12. Mean scores in reading, social studies, and to a lesser degree science declined from 1992 to 1993, but sharp increases in the following year more than offset those losses (Figure 11). Except in mathematics, most of the increase in scores—all of it in social studies—was concentrated in a single year, from 1993 to 1994.

These gains are so large that they raise the question of inflation, stemming either from misleadingly low initial scores or misleadingly high scores at the end of the time period. True gains in student performance of the magnitude of many of those shown here—such as mathematics in all three grades, science in grades 4 and 11/12, and especially reading in grade 4—would be very large for a large-scale and relatively short-term educational intervention. In an earlier section of this chapter, we evaluated the improvements set by the KIRIS thresholds by comparing them to other information on the distribution of student performance. The same criteria can be used here. The mean difference in eighth-grade mathematics scores on TIMSS between Japan (one of the highest-scoring countries) and the U.S. (which ranked 18th of the 25 nations with good samples) was about 1.1 standard deviations. In other words, if the observed gain in mathematics scores in any grade on KIRIS represented real, commensurate gains in learning, it would be roughly equivalent to

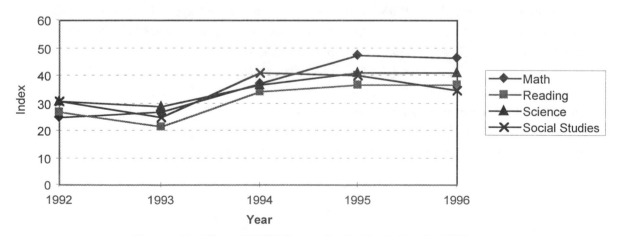

Figure 11—Mean KIRIS Scores by Subject, Grade 11/12

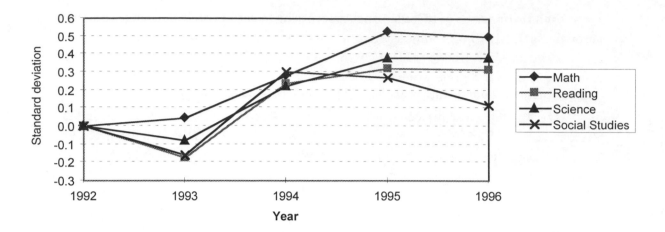

Figure 12—Cumulative Change in KIRIS Scores by Subject, Grade 11/12, in Standard Deviations

erasing about half of the difference between Japan and the U.S. in the space of only three years. Moreover, the observed gain on KIRIS in fourth-grade reading is more than twice as large as the gain in mathematics.

TRENDS IN THE PERCENTAGE OF STUDENTS REACHING PERFORMANCE LEVELS

When KIRIS began, the great majority of Kentucky students obtained scores of either Novice or Apprentice. A large share of the improvement in mean KIRIS scores over the first four years of the program reflects a rapid movement of students out of the Novice category and into the Apprentice category. Increases in the percentage of students scoring as Proficient were typically smaller, but in some cases they too contributed substantially to the increase in mean scores.

These patterns are clear in the trends in fourth-grade scores. In all subjects, the largest change from 1992 to 1995—1995 being the last year of the general increase in KIRIS scores—was the decrease in the percentage of students scored as Novice. The percentage of students scored as Novice dropped by 47 percentage points in reading, from 55 to 8 percent (Table 1).[6] The decrease was almost as striking in mathematics, from 70 percent Novice in 1992 to 29 percent in 1995. The decrease in Novice students was 31 percentage points in science and 14 percentage points in social studies. In mathematics and science, most of the offsetting change was a large increase in the percentage of students scoring at the Apprentice level. In reading, the increase in the percentage of students scored as Proficient was even

---

[6]The 1992 percentages displayed here are approximations. The only available scores for 1992 are based on the original KIRIS scaling method, which was dropped in 1995. Results for 1993 and 1994 were rescaled by KDE via the method used in 1995, but 1992 scores were not. Our 1992 percentages were estimated by subtracting the change from 1992 to 1993 on the older scale from 1993 percentages on the current scale.

larger than the increase in those scoring Apprentice. In social studies, the offsetting increase was primarily at the Proficient level, but it was much smaller in absolute terms.

Table 1

Percentage of Fourth-Grade Students at Each Performance Level, by Subject and Year

	1992	1995
Reading		
Novice	55	8
Apprentice	42	63
Proficient	3	28
Distinguished	0	2
Mathematics		
Novice	70	29
Apprentice	26	54
Proficient	3	10
Distinguished	2	8
Science		
Novice	59	28
Apprentice	39	67
Proficient	2	5
Distinguished	0	0
Social Studies		
Novice	46	32
Apprentice	47	51
Proficient	7	16
Distinguished	0	2

NOTE: Percentages may not sum to 100 because of rounding.

Grade 8 also showed large shifts out of the Novice category. Consistent with the smaller increase in means in grade 8 in most subjects, however, the shifts in the classifications of students were more modest than were those in the fourth grade. In reading, mathematics, and science, the largest change was the shrinkage of the Novice category, the bulk of which was absorbed by an increase in the Apprentice category (Table 2). Social studies was again an exception; the smaller decrease in the Novice category was largely offset by growth in the Proficient group.

In grade 11/12 as well, decreases in the Novice category were again the largest changes (Table 3). In reading and science, the offsetting increase was again clearly largest in the Apprentice group. In contrast, in mathematics, growth in the Proficient and Distinguished categories absorbed most of the shrinkage of the Novice group.[7]

---

[7]These tabulations understate slightly the changes in mathematics and reading because of the shift of testing in 1995 from grade 12 to grade 11. The decreases in average scores resulting from this change in procedures, however, were trivial in science and social studies and small in mathematics and reading and should have had only a minor impact on the percentages reported here.

Table 2

**Percentage of Eighth-Grade Students at Each Performance
Level, by Subject and Year**

	1992	1995
Reading		
Novice	22	7
Apprentice	72	80
Proficient	6	13
Distinguished	0	0
Mathematics		
Novice	64	36
Apprentice	24	35
Proficient	8	16
Distinguished	4	14
Science		
Novice	64	43
Apprentice	36	56
Proficient	1	2
Distinguished	0	0
Social Studies		
Novice	33	26
Apprentice	58	53
Proficient	9	18
Distinguished	0	3

NOTE: Percentages may not sum to 100 because of rounding.

RESULTS FROM THE 1997 ASSESSMENT

After holding nearly constant in 1996, average scores resumed their upward trend in 1997. The increases appeared in all grades and all four core subjects. The gains varied greatly in size but were in some cases comparable to or even greater than those experienced in earlier years.

Fourth-grade scores showed sizable increases in three subjects: 7.3 points in reading, 5.9 points in mathematics, and 8.3 points in science. The mean score in social studies changed little. In standardized terms, these one-year increases corresponded to 0.28 standard deviation in reading, 0.16 standard deviation in mathematics, and fully 0.36 standard deviation in science.

Mean scores in grade 8 increased by 3.7 points in reading, 6.5 points in mathematics, 5.0 points in science, and 3.1 points in social studies. In standardized terms, these increases were smaller than those in the fourth grade but were considerable for a single year nonetheless; they ranged from 0.09 standard deviation in social studies to 0.23 standard deviation in science.

Table 3

**Percentage of Eleventh/Twelfth-Grade Students at Each
Performance Level, by Subject and Year**

	1992	1995
Reading		
Novice	49	32
Apprentice	41	57
Proficient	10	10
Distinguished	1	1
Mathematics		
Novice	55	35
Apprentice	35	39
Proficient	7	17
Distinguished	3	9
Science		
Novice	32	16
Apprentice	63	72
Proficient	5	10
Distinguished	0	2
Social Studies		
Novice	42	30
Apprentice	46	52
Proficient	11	16
Distinguished	1	3

NOTE: Percentages may not sum to 100 because of rounding.

Overall, gains were greatest in the eleventh grade. The mean score increased by 5.9 points (0.14 standard deviation) in mathematics and 4.4 points (0.16 standard deviation) in science. The mean score in social studies increased by 9.7 points, fully 0.27 standard deviation. The mean in reading increased by 20.4 points, or 0.66 standard deviation—a truly remarkable change for a single year.

5. PAST REPORTS PERTAINING TO THE VALIDITY OF KIRIS GAINS

Two earlier reports explored the validity of KIRIS score gains during the first years of the KERA program. Both raised serious concerns about the meaningfulness of gains, and both bear on the interpretation of our findings.

THE OEA PANEL REPORT

In 1994, the Office of Educational Accountability, a support agency of the Kentucky General Assembly, empaneled a committee of six outside experts to evaluate the measurement quality of KIRIS (Hambleton, et al., 1995). The committee, referred to here as the OEA Panel, considered a variety of aspects of measurement quality, one of which was the validity of gains on KIRIS scores from the first administration in 1992 to the third administration in 1994. The OEA Panel report stressed the risk that score gains in high-stakes assessment programs could exaggerate actual improvements in student achievement and argued that the generalizability of performance to assessment tasks for which students had not specifically been coached is among the most important tests of the validity of gains. The Panel approached this question by comparing trends seen for KIRIS to those on the Trial State Assessment (TSA) of NAEP and the ACT (formerly American College Testing Program) college-admissions tests for the subset of Kentucky students who took both tests. The Panel argued that NAEP provides the strongest external criterion because the enabling statute required that the KIRIS assessment be linked to NAEP and the KIRIS assessment framework draws heavily on the NAEP framework.

The OEA Panel concluded that as of the 1994 administration of the KIRIS assessment, the results of these comparisons indicated substantial inflation of gains on KIRIS: "The Panel believes that the reported gains in scores on KIRIS substantially overstate improvements in student achievement. Indeed, it is not clear whether any appreciable, generalizable gains in achievement have been produced in some grades and subjects. The external evidence to which KIRIS scores can be compared fails to reflect the gains shown on KIRIS. It is important to note, however, that this external evidence is limited; it includes only a limited number of grades and subject areas, and it does not include direct assessments of writing, which is an area in which a positive effect of KIRIS might seem particularly likely" (Hambleton, et al., 1995, p. 8-2).

The OEA Panel's discussion of these issues, however, pertains only to the first years of the operation of KIRIS. More recent NAEP and ACT data are extensively discussed in Chapters 7 and 8.

THE RAND SURVEY OF KENTUCKY EDUCATORS

More recent but less direct evidence calling into question the validity of KIRIS gains was provided by a survey of representative samples of Kentucky principals and teachers that was carried out by RAND in the spring of 1995 (Koretz, Barron, Mitchell, and Stecher, 1996). Educators were asked detailed questions about three topics that bear on the validity of gains: the methods they used to prepare students for KIRIS, the administration of the KIRIS assessments, and their judgments about the causes of their own schools' gains in KIRIS scores. Survey data are subject to important caveats. For example, findings reflect only respondents' judgments and may also be subject to distortions, such as a bias toward socially desirable responses. Nonetheless, the findings are suggestive.

Educators reported relying on a wide variety of approaches to raising scores. Some of the approaches, if effective, would be expected to raise student performance in meaningful ways, and educators' use of them might constitute positive if indirect evidence of the validity of gains. For example, a large majority of principals reported giving teachers a "great deal" of encouragement to raise expectations for students, focus instruction more on higher-order thinking skills, and improve instruction more generally.

A large percentage of educators, however, also relied substantially on forms of test preparation that have the potential to create artifactual gains in scores. One approach was de-emphasizing aspects of the curriculum not emphasized on the test so as to focus more on material KIRIS emphasizes. Eighty-seven percent of fourth-grade teachers agreed (40 percent strongly) that KIRIS had caused some teachers to "de-emphasize or neglect untested subject areas," and about the same percentages of eighth-grade mathematics teachers agreed that KIRIS had caused some mathematics teachers to de-emphasize or neglect untested mathematics topics (Koretz, Barron, Mitchell, and Stecher, 1996).

A second method of preparing students was labeled "direct test preparation," defined as "giving students instruction on test-taking skills or practice on old assessment items or practice tests" (Koretz, Barron, Mitchell, and Stecher, 1996, p. 43). This term subsumes a wide range of activities that could contribute to both meaningful and misleading gains in scores. Emulation of old test items will generally inflate scores, but it can also be an appropriate way to focus attention on skills emphasized by KIRIS and may lead to real gains in proficiency. However, excessive focus on test content, test format, or test-taking skills can produce artifactual gains in scores, undermining the validity of gains. While the dividing line between appropriate and inappropriate test preparation is not always clear, the responses of Kentucky educators raise concerns:[1]

> Most teachers reported substantial reliance on [direct test preparation]. Almost all teachers (92 percent) reported focusing at least a moderate amount . . . on test-taking skills, and 48 percent reported focusing a great deal on them. . . . Seventy-seven percent of teachers reported focusing at least a moderate amount on practice tests and test-preparation materials, and 36 percent reported focusing a great deal on them. Moreover, virtually all teachers (98 percent) reported that students in their schools were given practice on the previous year's KIRIS common items at least occasionally, and about half reported that students were frequently given practice on them. . . . Most teachers (83 percent) reported that students in their schools are at least occasionally provided practice on items that are highly similar to the previous year's matrix items, and 40 percent

---

[1]To put these responses in context, it is important to note that KDE encourages the use of released common items in instruction but forbids the use of matrix items, which might be reused.

reported that such practice is frequent. (Koretz, Barron, Mitchell, and Stecher, 1996, p. 43)

While educators reported a mix of both desirable and more-questionable approaches to raising scores, their opinions about what worked—specifically, about the causes of the gains in their own schools—showed a lack of confidence in the meaningfulness of those gains:

> Although . . . most educators reported a strong emphasis on broad instructional changes in response to KIRIS, "broad improvements in knowledge and skills" was one of two factors cited *least* frequently by teachers as having contributed a great deal to their schools' KIRIS gains, along with increases in student motivation: Only 16 percent cited each of these factors. . . . "Improvements in students' mastery of knowledge and skills that are emphasized in KIRIS" were cited by almost as few teachers (24 percent). Cited most frequently as having contributed a great deal to KIRIS gains were "increased familiarity with the KIRIS assessments" (55 percent) and "work with practice tests and other preparation materials" (51 percent). . . . However, most Kentucky educators reported that improvements in knowledge and skills contributed at least a "moderate amount" to the KIRIS gains in their schools. (Koretz, Barron, Mitchell, and Stecher, 1996, pp. 48-49)

Table 4 summarizes the educators' responses when asked about factors that contributed a great deal to KIRIS gains in their schools.

Table 4

Percentage of Teachers and Principals Reporting That Each Factor Contributed "A Great Deal" to KIRIS Gains in Their Schools

	Teachers	Principals
Increased familiarity with KIRIS	55	56
Work with practice tests and preparation materials	51	43
Improved test-taking skills	34	22
Differences between cohorts	26	19
Improvements in knowledge and skills emphasized in KIRIS	24	34
Broad improvements in knowledge and skills	16	31
Increased student motivation	16	20

SOURCE: Koretz, Barron, Mitchell, and Stecher, 1996, Table 6.4.

Finally, an appreciable minority of teachers reported that they were aware of questionable or inappropriate test administration practices in their own schools (Table 5). Only a small percentage reported the most flagrant cheating: obtaining still-secure test items from the previous year's test. A sizable percentage, however, reported other questionable practices, such as rephrasing questions. It is not known how often teachers observed these practices or how many students were affected. Other evidence suggests that some of these practices may have occurred in the context of providing accommodations (in some instances, inappropriate or excessive accommodations) to students with disabilities (Koretz, 1997). It may be significant that a similar survey of teachers' responses to the lower-stakes state assessment program in Maryland found somewhat lower incidences of these practices (Koretz, Mitchell, Barron, and Keith, 1996).

Table 5

Percentage of Teachers Reporting Incidence of Questionable Test Preparation and Administration Practices

Practice	Yes	Occasionally or Frequently	Frequently
Obtained last year's nonreleased matrix items*	6		
Obtained student responses to last year's matrix items*	4		
Questions rephrased during testing time		36	12
Questions about content of assessment answered during testing time		21	6
Revisions recommended during or after assessment		21	6
Hints provided on correct answers		17	3
Changes or edits made to answers in assessment booklets		9	2
Items read for students		*43*	*2*
Responses written for students		*15*	*4*

NOTE: Items marked with an asterisk allowed only "yes" or "no" answers. In all other cases, respondents were allowed "never," "occasionally," or "frequently." Italicized items may pertain to students with special needs; see explanation in the text.

SOURCE: Koretz, Barron, Mitchell, and Stecher, 1996, Table 6.3.

6. EVIDENCE PERTAINING TO RETENTION IN GRADE

Scores on assessments can be inflated if educators exclude from the tested population students who are likely to score poorly. For example, Zlatos (1994), in a discussion of a testing program unrelated to KIRIS, noted that students with disabilities were excluded in some schools in order to raise scores. Similarly, students who are likely to score poorly can be retained in a lower grade so as to be excluded from testing until they are older and likely to score higher.

In the case of KIRIS, exclusion of students with disabilities is unlikely to pose a serious threat to the validity of gains. KDE regulations governing the inclusion of students with disabilities are among the strongest in the nation. In addition, Kentucky educators have a strong incentive to include most students with disabilities in the regular KIRIS assessment. Students who meet explicit requirements can be excluded from the regular KIRIS assessment and assessed with an "alternate portfolio," but these criteria are very stringent. Other students with disabilities are simply assigned a score of zero if they are not tested. Presumably because of these rules and incentives, the regular KIRIS assessment appears to include the large majority of identified students with disabilities (Koretz, 1997). However, educators could inflate KIRIS gains by retaining an increasing proportion of low-achieving students in grade and then testing them when they are a year or two older.

KDE collects data on retention rates as an element of the noncognitive component of its accountability index. These data are not ideal for measuring trends, however. They reflect the percentage of students in all grades in a school retained in a given year, rather than the percentage of students who are retained at least once. Moreover, the system for collecting retention (and other noncognitive) data has been evolving, raising the possibility that changes in reporting could have distorted trends in retention rates.

KDE reported some increase in retention rates between 1992 and 1995, but it was trivial except at the senior-high level. In grades 4 and 8, the statewide reported retention rate increased by less than half a percentage point; in grade 11/12, the retention rate increased by a little more than one percentage point (Table 6).[1]

Table 6

**Percentage of Students Reported as Retained in Grade,
by Grade and Year**

Grade	1993	1994	1995
4	0.7	0.6	1.1
8	1.4	1.6	1.74
11/12	5.1	5.3	6.4

SOURCE: Kentucky Department of Education, 1996b.

---

[1]Retention data for 1996 were not yet available when this report was written.

To avoid the weaknesses of this retention measure, we calculated the age distribution of students tested in the fourth and eighth grades in the years from 1992 through 1996. The age distribution is a more sensitive measure because it captures the cumulative effects of all placement and retention decisions from the date of a student's initial entry into school. Moreover, the age distribution, unlike KDE's retention measure, is not vulnerable to changes in schools' reporting practices.

Trends in the age distribution for students tested in grades four and eight show no indication that educators held students back to increase gains on KIRIS. The age distribution of students tested in the eighth grade scarcely changed from 1992 through 1996. The modal age of students tested was 14 in all four years. Fourteen-year-olds constituted 66 percent of those tested when KIRIS was first administered in 1992; from 1994 through 1996, they constituted about 69 percent. The percentage of tested eighth graders who were above the modal age of 14 declined slightly, from about 33 percent in 1992 to about 30 percent from 1994 to 1996. Only about 1 percent of those tested in any year were below the modal age of 14.

In contrast, the age distribution of students tested in the fourth grade changed appreciably, but in a manner that would depress rather than inflate score gains (Table 7). That is, tested students became appreciably younger over the four-year period from 1992 to 1996. Ten-year-olds are the modal group; they increased from 71 to 79 percent of those tested between 1992 and 1996. Students above the modal age of 10 decreased from 29 percent to 20 percent of those tested over the same period. About 1 percent of those tested in each year were below the modal age of 10.

Table 7

Percentage of Tested Fourth Graders in Four Age Groups, 1992-96

Age	Year				
	1992	1993	1994	1995	1996
Under 10	0.7	0.7	1.1	1.0	1.0
10	70.6	71.7	74.3	77.5	78.5
11	25.2	24.9	22.6	19.9	19.0
Over 11	3.4	2.7	2.1	1.6	1.5

NOTE: 1992 through 1995 figures reflect RAND calculations; 1996 figures were provided by KDE. All figures exclude students (up to 4.4 percent of those tested) with unusable date-of-birth information.

7. EXTERNAL EVIDENCE FROM NAEP

The National Assessment of Educational Progress provides a particularly important external criterion for evaluating gains on KIRIS. NAEP is a nationally recognized indicator of student performance. It is administered under controlled and secure conditions, and it is largely unaffected by the potential for inflated score gains. On several occasions, it has been administered to large, representative samples in many states, including Kentucky.

In addition, the frameworks for the KIRIS assessments were strongly influenced by NAEP's frameworks. The first KIRIS technical report stated that "the [Kentucky] valued outcomes, as supplemented by frameworks from the National Assessment of Educational Progress (NAEP), will determine what is to be assessed and how it is to be assessed. . . . Using the NAEP frameworks as a supplement to the valued outcomes also ensured that the Kentucky tests could be compared to NAEP. . . . Kentucky's reading framework [is] similar to that of the 1992 NAEP framework. . . . The entire [mathematics] framework is consistent with the most recent NAEP framework for mathematics" (Kentucky Department of Education, 1993a, pp. 4, 14, 17). This similarity is unusual among state testing programs. For example, shortly after the inception of KIRIS, Bond and Jaeger (1993, p. 447) noted that "an opportunity to replicate this study [of the congruence between state assessments in mathematics and NAEP] using at least one state assessment test that is very similar to the NAEP mathematics item pool in its content distribution is likely to arise. . . . The state of Kentucky has, for the first time, administered an assessment test that is modeled after the NAEP mathematics item pool."

Thus, a substantial degree of congruence between KIRIS and NAEP was intended from the outset of the KIRIS program. The two assessments could still look quite different, because the authors of the tests might select tasks differently from each category of the framework, choose different styles of tasks, write tasks at different levels of difficulty, and so on. Actual similarities and differences between the two assessments, which are discussed below, may be helpful in explaining any lack of generalizability of performance from one assessment to the other. In one sense, however, the similarity of the frameworks is even more important for the validation of gains, because the frameworks represent the *inferences the assessment is designed to support*, and the reasonableness of those inferences is the core question of validity.

Thus, if the gains on KIRIS represent generalizable improvements in students' knowledge and skills, they should be reflected in NAEP data. If the gains on both assessments stemmed from teachers' responses to KIRIS, gains on NAEP would likely be smaller than those on KIRIS because even tests built from similar frameworks differ in coverage and emphasis. Moreover, the tests differ in numerous other respects, so small differences between the trends shown by the two tests would be hard to interpret. Nonetheless, it seems reasonable to expect an appreciable reflection of the KIRIS gains in the NAEP data.

One factor that complicates comparison of KIRIS to NAEP is that the two assessments differ substantially in format. Although NAEP has increased its use of constructed-response items, much of the assessment remains multiple choice, and many of its constructed-response tasks have entailed only short prompts and short responses. In contrast, KIRIS has always stressed constructed-response tasks, and in 1995, it included no multiple-choice items at all. Thus it is possible that NAEP contains too few constructed-response items, or too few tasks that are sufficiently large in scale, to mirror fully improvements in the skills measured by KIRIS.

The comparison between NAEP and KIRIS is also complicated by several differences that make it difficult to place the trends in a comparable metric. Trends on both tests were standardized for the analyses reported here, but these standardized scores are not completely comparable. One reason is that one of the assessments may include more measurement error, which would inflate the standard deviation of scores (the denominator of the standardized scores) and therefore make standardized gains on that assessment appear smaller. For example, the lack of consequences for NAEP scores could affect the motivation of some students more than others, increasing the standard deviation of scores.[1] However, NAEP scores are "conditioned" to remove measurement error (e.g., Mislevy, 1992), which decreases the standard deviation of scores.

More important, the KIRIS scores for 1992—which were needed for comparison of KIRIS and NAEP (and ACT—see Chapter 8) trends—were only available on the ordinal, four-point NAPD (Novice, Apprentice, Proficient, Distinguished) scale. For all of our analyses, these scores were given the same values assigned in the Kentucky accountability index (Novice=0, Apprentice=40, Proficient=100, and Distinguished=140) and then standardized. This standardization is inherently ambiguous, but comparison to a continuous scale available since 1993 suggests that the result is a modest understatement of the discrepancy between KIRIS and NAEP (see Appendix).

NAEP trends for Kentucky are available for fourth-grade reading comparing 1992 to 1994—the first two years of the KIRIS program—and for fourth- and eighth-grade mathematics comparing 1992 to 1996.

READING: THE OEA ANALYSIS

The contrast between KIRIS and NAEP trends in fourth-grade reading for 1992 to 1994 was one of the primary reasons for the OEA Panel's conclusion that "gains in KIRIS scores [were] substantially inflated [between 1992 and 1994] and provide the public with a misleading view of improvements in student performance" (Hambleton, et al., 1995, p. 8-4). (The state-level NAEP assessment in 1994 included only fourth-grade reading.) The panel noted: "First, the statewide average fourth grade KIRIS reading score roughly doubled between 1992 and 1994. . . . The KIRIS gain corresponds to about three-fourths of a standard deviation, which is a very large impact compared to those commonly found in large-scale educational interventions. . . . In contrast, the Kentucky statewide fourth-grade average on

---

[1]The authors are indebted to Laurie Wise for pointing out this possibility.

NAEP remained virtually unchanged" (Hambleton, et al., 1995, p. 8-8). The Panel also noted that the disparity in change was particularly pronounced at the low end of the distribution, as indicated by the percentage of students reaching the Apprentice standard, but was apparent at the high end of the distribution (above Proficient) as well.

The lack of change in Kentucky's NAEP reading scores between 1992 and 1994 makes this comparison particularly clear. If NAEP scores had risen, but markedly less than KIRIS scores, one would face the uncertain judgment of how much of an echo of KIRIS gains to expect in the results of other tests. However, the short time span in this comparison—the data available to the OEA Panel spanned only the first few years of KERA and the first three administrations of KIRIS—limits the implications of the disparity in the two trends. Even if the gains on KIRIS during its first years are attributable to factors such as familiarization rather than growth in the knowledge and skills it is intended to measure, later increases in scores might reflect generalizable gains in student performance. More-recent NAEP data unfortunately are not available for reading, but they are available for mathematics.

MATHEMATICS

Data on NAEP trends for mathematics in Kentucky became available in 1997 (Reese, Miller, Mazzeo, and Dossey, 1997). These data reflect fourth- and eighth-grade NAEP assessments conducted in the state in 1992 and 1996.

Kentucky's public-school students showed substantial and statistically significant gains on the NAEP mathematics assessment in both grades, comparable to the average gains in the nation as a whole. These gains were much smaller, however, than were the corresponding gains on KIRIS, and their causes are uncertain.

The following discussion of NAEP data is broken into three sections. The first describes the NAEP and KIRIS mathematics frameworks and presents some items from each assessment to illustrate similarities and differences between them. The next section compares the magnitude of KIRIS gains to those on NAEP within Kentucky. To provide a perspective for these comparisons, the final section compares NAEP trends in Kentucky to those nationwide.

Similarities and Differences Between the NAEP and KIRIS Mathematics Assessments

The degree of similarity between NAEP and KIRIS is important because it influences the amount of echo of KIRIS gains one expects to find in NAEP scores if KIRIS gains are a valid indicator of improved student learning. Some observers argue that one should find a substantial echo. They note that the KIRIS assessments were claimed to mirror the NAEP frameworks, and they argue that few stakeholders would be satisfied if KERA were creating changes in student performance so specific that they did not appear in NAEP. Indeed, KERA was clearly instituted with the expectation that improvements would be echoed in NAEP. Others argue that differences between the assessments in both content and format are so large that a marked divergence between the trends is reasonable.

The framework of the KIRIS mathematics assessment overlaps a great deal with that of NAEP, as the designers of KIRIS intended. NAEP delineates five content areas within mathematics:

- number sense, properties, and operations;
- measurement;
- geometry;
- data analysis, statistics, and probability; and
- algebra and functions.

The KIRIS framework specifies seven content areas (see Kentucky Department of Education, 1995b, pp. 23-34):

- number;
- mathematical procedures;
- space and dimensionality;
- measurement;
- change;
- mathematical structure; and
- data.

Together, the first two content categories in the KIRIS framework are similar to NAEP's first category: number sense, properties, and operations. The space and dimensionality area contains, among other things, regular and irregular figures, similarity, and congruence; it seems reasonable to consider the combination of this category and measurement to be similar to the combination of NAEP's geometry and measurement categories. Much of what NAEP could classify as algebra and functions, such as functions, variables, and algebraic representations, appears in KIRIS's change category. The KIRIS data category, like the NAEP data analysis, statistics, and probability category, includes statistical procedures and probability.

NAEP crosses its five content categories with three cognitive processes: conceptual understanding, procedural knowledge, and problem solving. KIRIS specifies these same three processes as well as a fourth, reasoning and analysis (Kentucky Department of Education, 1993a, p. 17).

We did not conduct a complete mapping of the two assessments to detail similarities and differences in content; this appears unnecessary given the similarities in the inferences intended by the two assessments and the magnitude of the disparities in the trends they showed. However, we did examine all KIRIS test items in mathematics for all years through 1995, and we compared them to publicly released items from the 1996 NAEP assessment. That examination suggested some similarities and differences in both content and format that provide a useful context for interpreting the divergences in trends described below.

As noted earlier, the two assessments differ in their mix of formats despite their similar frameworks. Although multiple-choice items were not counted in the KIRIS accountability index, they were included in the assessment in 1992, not included in 1995, and then reintroduced in 1997. NAEP still relies substantially on multiple-choice items, but it also includes both short and extended constructed-response items. This format difference, however, should not be overstated. First, NAEP does include open-response items, and some of them require extended constructed responses and substantial use of language. Three examples from the 1996 fourth-grade NAEP are shown in Figure 13. Second, while some KIRIS test items do require extended responses, others do not. Some items require, for example, simple calculations to solve conventional word problems of the sort that are often presented either as multiple-choice or short-answer questions on other assessments, including NAEP. KIRIS items, however, often add to these tasks the requirement that students explain their answers. Figure 14 shows a fourth-grade KIRIS item that requires an explanation, along with an eighth-grade item of the same type that does not require an

Think carefully about the following question. Write a complete answer. You may use drawings, words, and numbers to explain your answer. Be sure to show all of your work.

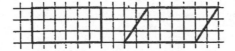

10. In what ways are the figures above alike?   List as many ways as you can.

In what ways are the figures above different?   List as many ways as you can.

Q001390

8. Brett needs to cut a piece of string into four equal pieces without using a ruler or other measuring instrument.

Write directions to tell Brett how to do this.

_____

_____

_____

_____

EL001540

Figure 13—NAEP Grade 4 Mathematics Items 12-8, 12-9, 9-10

Think carefully about the following question. Write a complete answer. You may use drawings, words, and numbers to explain your answer. Be sure to show all of your work.

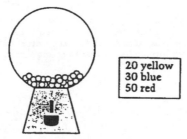

20 yellow
30 blue
50 red

9. The gum ball machine has 100 gum balls; 20 are yellow, 30 are blue, and 50 are red. The gum balls are well mixed inside the machine.

Jenny gets 10 gum balls from this machine.

What is your best prediction of the number that will be red?

Answer: _____ gum balls

Explain why you chose this number.

_____

_____

_____

_____

_____

Figure 13 (continued)

35. Mr. Miller's class is having a bake sale to raise money for a class trip. Each student offered to bake one batch of a different kind of cookie for the sale. By the day of the sale, the students had baked 550 cookies. The class is thinking about charging 15¢ per cookie. They hope to raise $100.

a. If Mr. Miller's class sold every cookie they baked for 15¢, how much money would they earn? Would they make as much money as they hoped to make? Explain your answer.

b. Some students think the cookies should be sold for 20¢ each. How much money would the class earn if they sold every cookie they baked for 20¢? Explain what you did to get your answer.

c. Imagine that Mr. Miller's class could predict that they would only sell 400 cookies. What price would they have to charge to raise $100? Explain how you got your answer.

35. A hot new rock group is coming to Kentucky for two performances. The concerts will be held at Rupp Arena, which has a seating capacity of 24,000, and Freedom Hall, which has a seating capacity of 19,000. The group needs to make $150,000 from each concert to cover their expenses. They would like to make a total profit of $110,000. It is predicted that 75% of the tickets will sell. The cost of the tickets needs to be the same at both arenas. What would be the minimum cost of the tickets, to the nearest dollar? Show how you arrived at your answer.

Figure 14—KIRIS Grade 4 Mathematics Item 14 and Grade 8 Mathematics Item 33

explanation. Figure 15 shows a fourth-grade NAEP item that presents a computational word problem and requires a short constructed response but no explanation.

7. Sam can purchase his lunch at school. Each day he wants to have juice that costs 50¢, a sandwich that costs 90¢, and fruit that costs 35¢. His mother has only $1.00 bills. What is the least number of $1.00 bills that his mother should give him so he will have enough money to buy lunch for 5 days?

AP000522

Figure 15—NAEP Grade 4 Mathematics Item 12-7

These examples also show that there is clear overlap in content between the two assessments. Both include, for example, tasks that would be classified by NAEP as numbers and operations; measurement; and data analysis, statistics, and probability. At the same time, there are differences as well, although it is not clear whether these represent planned differences in content or unrelated aspects of test construction. For example, Figure 16 shows a sample of the fourth-grade KIRIS questions involving evaluation and extension of numerical series. Three of 15 reused items in the 1995 fourth-grade KIRIS assessment were of this type. While items of this type are used in NAEP as well, they make up a much larger share of the KIRIS assessment.

2. The libraries at Lincoln School and King School both charge their students fines for overdue books.

Fines at Lincoln School

Number of Days Overdue	1	2	3	4	and so on
Fine	15¢	23¢	31¢	39¢	and so on

Fines at King School

Number of Days Overdue	1	2	3	4	and so on
Fine	1¢	2¢	4¢	8¢	and so on

a. If you returned a book to Lincoln School that was 5 days overdue, how much would your fine be? Explain how you figured this out.

b. If you returned a book to King School that was 5 days overdue, how much would your fine be? Explain how you figured this out.

c. Kendra and Brian are each returning a book that is 8 days overdue. Kendra's book is from the Lincoln School library, while Brian's book is from the King School library. Who will pay the greater fine? Explain how you figured this out.

BE SURE TO LABEL YOUR RESPONSES (a), (b), AND (c).

Figure 16—KIRIS Grade 4 Mathematics Item 35, 1995

A few KIRIS items appear qualitatively more distinct from those in NAEP. One example is a spatial visualization task used in grade 8 in 1993, 1994, and 1995 (Figure 17). While there was little change in performance for this task from 1993 to 1994, there was a very large gain in 1995, larger than for any other reused item. This large change did not contribute to the gain in average scores in 1995. The item was moved from the back to the front of a form when it became a common item in 1995, so it was treated as a new item in 1995 and not equated. Thus, it could contribute to the *relative* gains shown by different schools but not to the overall gain statewide. Nonetheless, the large gain is noteworthy and is revisited in Chapter 10. One other task from the same assessment that also appeared qualitatively distinct to us cannot be described here because it was never released by KDE.

2. Here are the designs drawn on the six faces of a cube.

Here are three views of a **closed cube.**

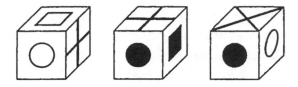

a. Which design is on the face opposite the open circle?

b. Draw an **open view** of the cube (which means that when the cube is flattened you can view each face of the cube) in your Student Response Booklet. Label each face with the appropriate design.

c. Design a cube of your own. In your Student Response Booklet, draw a closed view of your cube with three faces labeled. Draw an open view of the same cube with all six faces labeled.

Figure 17—KIRIS Grade 8 Mathematics Item 20, 1995

Gains on KIRIS Compared to Kentucky's Gains on NAEP

As noted earlier, statewide average KIRIS scores rose rapidly from 1992 to 1995 in both fourth and eighth grade (Figures 7 and 9). In 1996, scores leveled off in grade 8 and actually declined slightly in grade 4. Despite these changes, the average on the accountability index scale doubled in grade 4 over the four-year period and nearly doubled in grade 8. These gains can be compared to Kentucky's improvement in NAEP scores by standardizing the gain on each test relative to the standard deviations of students' scores on that test.

Kentucky's average increase on the fourth-grade NAEP from 1992 to 1996, 0.17 standard deviation, was sizable for such a short time (Table 8). One standard of comparison suggested earlier for gauging the size of trends is the magnitude of the drop in average scores during the achievement decline of the 1960s and 1970s, a trend that appears to have resulted from broad societal changes as well as educational policies and practices (Koretz, 1987). During that period, the average score on most tests dropped by less than 0.4 standard deviation, and the drop on some tests was considerably smaller (Koretz, 1986). Thus, the increase in NAEP scores in Kentucky from 1992 to 1996 was roughly half as large as the drop in scores during the decade-long achievement decline.

Table 8

Kentucky's Gains in Fourth-Grade Mathematics, KIRIS and NAEP, 1992-96

	KIRIS	NAEP
Raw Gain	22.9	5
Standardized Gain	0.61	0.17
Ratio, KIRIS to NAEP		3.6

Kentucky's fourth-grade gain on KIRIS, however, was roughly four times as large as the corresponding gain on NAEP. While Kentucky's gain on NAEP was 0.17 standard deviation, the gain on KIRIS over the four-year period was 0.61 standard deviation, 3.6 times the size of the gain on NAEP. Moreover, the increase in KIRIS scores over the three-year period from 1992 to 1995 was even larger: 0.69 standard deviation, 4.1 times the four-year gain on NAEP. This gain was partially offset by a small decline in KIRIS scores from 1995 to 1996.

Eighth grade showed an even more striking contrast: the gain on KIRIS from 1992 to 1996 was more than four times as large as that on NAEP. The raw gain on KIRIS was 23.7 points on the index, corresponding to a standardized increase of 0.56 standard deviation (Table 9). Kentucky's mean gain on NAEP in the eighth grade was 0.13 standard deviation, slightly smaller than in the fourth grade. Thus, the gain on KIRIS over the four-year period was 4.1 times as large as the gain on NAEP. The three-year gain on KIRIS from 1992 to 1995 was 4.4 times as large as the four-year gain on NAEP; again, this KIRIS gain was partially offset by a small decrease from 1995 to 1996.

Table 9

Kentucky's Gains in Eighth-Grade Mathematics, KIRIS and NAEP, 1992-96

	KIRIS	NAEP
Raw Gain	23.7	4
Standardized Gain	0.52	0.13
Ratio, KIRIS to NAEP		4.1

As noted earlier, much of the change in KIRIS scores reflects movement of students out of the lowest level (Novice) or the lowest two levels (Novice and Apprentice). These changes were much larger than the corresponding changes in the performance of Kentucky students with respect to the NAEP standards. In 1992, the lowest Kentucky performance standard, Apprentice (which divides the Apprentice from the Novice level) was more difficult for Kentucky students than the lowest NAEP standard, Basic. For example, of Kentucky fourth-grade students in 1992, only 34 percent scored at the Apprentice level or above in KIRIS mathematics, in contrast to 51 percent who scored at the Basic level or above on

NAEP mathematics (Table 10). The percentage reaching the lowest standard increased much more rapidly on KIRIS than on NAEP, however, and by 1996, more students reached the KIRIS Apprentice level than the NAEP Basic level. In the fourth grade, the percentage of students reaching or exceeding the KIRIS Apprentice level more than doubled, from 34 to 71 percent. Over the same period, the percentage of students reaching the NAEP Basic level increased only from 51 to 60 percent. The differential was less marked but still striking in grade 8: far more students moved out of the lowest level on KIRIS than on NAEP.

Table 10

Percentage of Students At or Above the Lowest Standard in Mathematics, KIRIS and Kentucky NAEP, 1992 and 1996

	1992	1996
Fourth Grade		
KIRIS: Apprentice	34	71
NAEP: Basic	51	60
Eighth Grade		
KIRIS: Apprentice	38	64
NAEP: Basic	43	51

SOURCES: RAND tabulations; Kentucky Department of Education, 1996b, Table 7; Reese, Miller, Mazzeo, and Dossey, 1997. KIRIS results reflect open-response test items only.

The contrast between KIRIS and NAEP trends was less pronounced but still sizable at the Proficient level—the name given to the second-highest standard in both assessments. In 1992, the fourth grade Proficient standard was more difficult in KIRIS than in NAEP; 13 percent of Kentucky students reached or exceeded that standard in NAEP, compared to 5 percent in KIRIS (Table 11). By 1996, however, the percentage of fourth-grade students reaching or exceeding this level on KIRIS nearly tripled, to 14 percent, while the percentage reaching or exceeding it on NAEP increased more modestly, to 16 percent. In grade 8, the percentage reaching or exceeding these standards increased from 12 to 28 percent on KIRIS but from 10 to 14 percent on NAEP.

Table 11

Percentage of Students At or Above the Proficient Standard in Mathematics, KIRIS and Kentucky NAEP, 1992 and 1996

	1992	1996
Fourth Grade		
KIRIS	5	14
NAEP	13	16
Eighth Grade		
KIRIS	12	28
NAEP	10	14

SOURCES: RAND tabulations; Kentucky Department of Education, 1996b, Table 7; Reese, Miller, Mazzeo, and Dossey, 1997. KIRIS results reflect open-response test items only.

Kentucky's NAEP Trends Compared to the Nation's

A comparison of NAEP trends in Kentucky and elsewhere may also contribute validity evidence, depending on the inferences users draw. For example, if users infer that Kentucky's NAEP gains were a result of the KERA reforms and are thus an echo of gains on KIRIS, it would be informative to see whether Kentucky's gains on NAEP were unusually large compared to NAEP gains elsewhere. By the same token, the possibility of some NAEP gains not generalizing to KIRIS (area D in Figure 6, above) might seem more likely if Kentucky's NAEP gains reflected nationwide changes (either in educational practice or in noneducational factors that influence performance).

Among public-school students in grades 4 and 8, Kentucky's gains on the NAEP mathematics assessment were similar to those in the nation as a whole. In fourth grade, Kentucky showed a gain of five points on the NAEP scale between 1992 and 1996, while the national mean increased by four points. In eighth grade, this trivial difference was reversed: scores increased by four points in Kentucky and by five points in the nation as a whole (Reese, Miller, Mazzeo, and Dossey, 1997, Tables 2.2 and 2.3).

That Kentucky's NAEP gains are typical of the nation becomes even more apparent when they are compared to the distribution of gains of all states that participated in the NAEP Trial State Assessment in both 1992 and 1996 (39 states in grade 4 and 38 in grade 8). In grade 8, there was remarkably little variation among states in the gains: 31 of 38 participating states had gains within two points of Kentucky's four-point gain. This comparison is shown graphically in Figure 18, in which the mean change in each participating state is shown by a single dot. Eight states, including Kentucky, showed an increase of four points; nine states showed an increase of five points, which was the national change in mean scores.

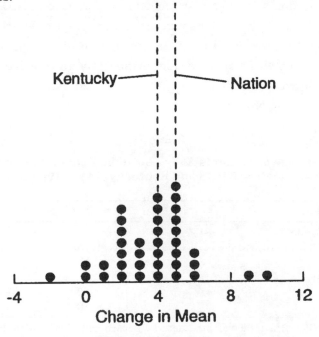

Figure 18—Mean Change in NAEP Mathematics for States, Grade 8, 1992-96

Gains in the fourth grade varied somewhat more, but many states were still clustered closely around the gains shown by Kentucky and by the nation as a whole. Fifteen states (39 percent of the 39 states) had gains within two points of Kentucky's, and 26 (67 percent) showed gains within three points of Kentucky's (Figure 19).

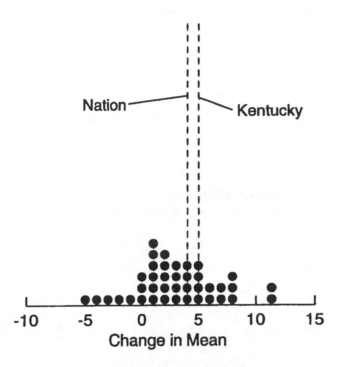

Figure 19—Mean Change in NAEP Mathematics for States, Grade 4, 1992-96

This similarity of gains across states is even more striking when sampling and measurement error are considered. In the eighth grade, for example, a confidence interval of two standard errors around the estimated change in the median state was ± 3.6 points—a range wide enough to encompass the majority of states. Thus, Kentucky's change on NAEP is not reliably different from that of the nation as a whole or of most other states participating in the Trial State Assessment.

Kentucky and the nation also showed similar improvement in the percentage of students reaching or exceeding NAEP's Proficient standard, the second-highest of NAEP's achievement levels (Table 12). However, Kentucky did show somewhat more improvement than the nation as a whole in the percentage of students reaching or exceeding NAEP's Basic achievement level (Table 13). This improvement may be a modest echo of the much larger increases (described above) in the percentages of Kentucky students scoring at or above the KIRIS Apprentice level.

Table 12

**Percentage Reaching or Exceeding the NAEP Proficient
Standard, Kentucky and the Nation**

	1992	1996	Gain
Grade 4			
Kentucky	13	16	3
Nation	17	20	3
Grade 8			
Kentucky	10	14	4
Nation	15	20	5

SOURCE: Reese, Miller, Mazzeo, and Dossey, 1997, Tables 3.2 and 3.3.

Table 13

**Percentage Reaching or Exceeding the NAEP Basic
Standard, Kentucky and the Nation**

	1992	1996	Gain
Grade 4			
Kentucky	51	60	9
Nation	57	62	5
Grade 8			
Kentucky	43	51	8
Nation	51	56	5

SOURCE: Reese, Miller, Mazzeo, and Dossey, 1997, Tables
3.2 and 3.3.

8. EXTERNAL EVIDENCE FROM THE ACT

Comparisons of ACT and KIRIS data are subject to several caveats that do not apply to NAEP-KIRIS comparisons, but they are informative nonetheless. As noted earlier, the OEA Panel analyzed ACT data in evaluating KIRIS gains through 1994. More extensive analyses of Kentucky's ACT data through 1995 are reported here following a summary of the OEA Panel's findings.

One limitation of the comparison of KIRIS and ACT scores is the fact that the ACT is taken by an unrepresentative, self-selected group of students, primarily those interested in applying for admission to four-year colleges. It is therefore necessary to take into account the possibility that the KIRIS trends of students taking the ACT may be unlike those in the state as a whole, or that changes in self-selection over time might bias comparisons.

Although the KIRIS trends of students who took the ACT were fairly similar to those of all students (see Appendix), all our analyses comparing the ACT to KIRIS were conducted with a special subsample created to minimize the effects of selection. Students were included in this subsample only if they took both the ACT and KIRIS and attended schools in which more than ten students took both tests.[1] KIRIS trends reported in this chapter have been recomputed to reflect only those students. This approach eliminates potential bias in the comparison of ACT and KIRIS scores but does not alter the fact that students taking the ACT are not fully representative of the state as a whole. These students have higher average scores than do other students and showed somewhat larger changes in average KIRIS scores. Thus, one cannot assume that results found with students taking the ACT would necessarily generalize fully to other students. Students taking the ACT do, however, constitute about half of all students taking KIRIS, so statewide trends in senior-high KIRIS scores are in substantial part a reflection of students who took the ACT as well.[2] The Appendix discusses the approaches we took to address this and other methodological issues that arose in comparing ACT and KIRIS scores.

A less substantial complication is that KIRIS testing was moved from grade 12 to grade 11 in 1995. Thus, 1995 KIRIS scores must be adjusted to place them on the scale used previously for twelfth-grade students. This adjustment, which is based on an equating study carried out by KDE, is also described in the Appendix.

The final and important caveat concerning comparisons of ACT and KIRIS trends is that the ACT differs considerably from KIRIS, notably more than NAEP does. Unlike KIRIS and NAEP, the ACT is entirely multiple choice. Moreover, unlike NAEP, it did not serve as a basis for constructing the KIRIS assessment framework. Because of these differences in the

---

[1]Students in schools in which fewer than ten students took both tests were excluded. Many of our analyses were conducted at the level of schools, and estimates for schools with few matched students would be unstable.

[2]Specifically, students who took the ACT, had matched KIRIS records, and attended schools in which more than ten students had such matched records constituted from 50 to 57 percent of all students taking KIRIS over the period from 1992 through 1995.

measurement goals of the ACT and KIRIS, it might be reasonable to expect somewhat greater divergence between ACT and KIRIS trends than between NAEP and KIRIS trends, even if there is no inflation of gains on KIRIS.

Nonetheless, it is reasonable to expect that KIRIS gains will be reflected in ACT trends to an appreciable degree. The domains of measurement of the two assessments overlap substantially, and as noted below, scores on the two assessments do show moderate to high correlations, particularly in mathematics. Moreover, KDE has used the correlations between scores on the ACT and KIRIS assessments as evidence of the validity of the KIRIS results and has predicted that gains on one test would generalize to the other. In the most recent KIRIS technical report, KDE wrote:

> In addition to providing concurrent validity evidence, a good reason for comparing KIRIS to traditional forms of assessment is that those traditional measures are still in use. Tens of thousands of Kentucky high school students will take the ACT each year for some time to come for college admissions. If KIRIS proved to be uncorrelated with that measure, it would place students, parents, and teachers in the uncomfortable position of having to choose the test on which they would like to focus their attention. Fortunately, as shown in the KIRIS Accountability Cycle 1 Technical Manual, there is significant correlation between KIRIS and ACT scores, and *it is not overly presumptuous to assume that increased learning that leads to improvement on one is likely to lead to improvement on the other.* (Kentucky Department of Education, 1997, p. 14-7, emphasis added)

Thus, regardless of concrete differences between the two assessments, the intended inferences from KIRIS overlap considerably with those from the ACT, and comparisons between them are a reasonable source of evidence of the validity of gains.

SIMILARITIES AND DIFFERENCES BETWEEN THE ACT AND KIRIS MATHEMATICS ASSESSMENTS

As noted earlier, the similarity of the intended domains of inference for two tests is in some respects more important for our purposes than are the concrete similarities and differences between the tests themselves. Nonetheless, it is still important to examine the assessments themselves so as to better understand any lack of generalizability of performance.

In this section, we describe similarities and differences between the ACT and KIRIS mathematics assessments. Clear differences among tests are likely to be larger and more apparent in content-rich areas such as mathematics than in reading, and the demands of assessment tasks are likely to be clearer.

The ACT and KIRIS assessments differ in numerous respects with regard to content, although less so than the simplest level of specifications might suggest. Specifications for the ACT mathematics test classify items into five content areas (see American College Testing, 1989):

- pre-algebra;
- elementary algebra;
- intermediate algebra and coordinate geometry;

- plane geometry; and
- trigonometry.

As noted earlier, seven content areas are specified for the KIRIS assessment:

- number;
- mathematical procedures;
- space and dimensionality;
- measurement;
- change;
- mathematical structure; and
- data.

At first glance, these content areas appear to overlap relatively little, but a more detailed examination of the specifications reveals considerable overlap in the material subsumed by them. For example, the ACT pre-algebra category includes "basic operations using whole numbers, decimals, and integers; place value; square roots and approximations; . . . factors; ratio, proportion, and percent; linear equations in one variable; absolute value and ordering numbers by value; [and] elementary counting techniques" (American College Testing, 1989, p. 7). The number and mathematical procedures categories in the KIRIS specifications overlap considerably with this and include number relations, estimation, percents, proportion, "computational algorithms," and "algebraic processes" (Kentucky Department of Education, 1993a, p. 19).

The elementary algebra and intermediate algebra content areas constitute roughly one-third of the ACT test. The description of these areas notes considerable detail and appears to reflect typical coursework for college-bound students taking several years of high school mathematics. For example, the specifications include "exponents and square roots, evaluation of algebraic expressions through substitution, . . . the solution of quadratic equations by factoring, . . . rational and radical expressions, absolute value equations and inequalities, sequences and patterns, systems of equations, functions, modeling, matrices, roots of polynomials, and complex numbers" (American College Testing, 1989, p. 7). The KIRIS specifications do not include a specific algebra category and contain less detail in this area, but many of the elements of the ACT algebra specifications are noted in the mathematical procedures, change, and mathematical structure categories. These include algebraic processes, algebraic representations, functions, sequences, series, matrices, systems of equations, and inequalities (Kentucky Department of Education, 1993a, p. 19).

The plane and coordinate geometry categories constitute roughly another third of the ACT assessment in mathematics. Here again, the specifications are quite detailed and appear to mirror the typical content of upper-level coursework. They include, for example, "the relations between equations and graphs, including points, lines, polynomials, circles, and other curves; graphing inequalities; slope; parallel and perpendicular lines; distance; midpoints; . . . the properties of plane figures, including angles . . . ; properties of circles,

triangles, rectangles, parallelograms, and trapezoids; transformations; the concept of proof
. . . ; volume; and applications of geometry to three dimensions" (American College Testing,
1989, pp. 7-8). The KIRIS space and dimensionality and measurement categories include
some of these topics, albeit specified in less detail, such as coordinate systems, congruence,
similarity, "regular and irregular figures in various dimensions," and angle (Kentucky
Department of Education, 1993a, p. 19). The KIRIS measurement category also includes
numerous topics that are not specifically noted in the ACT specifications, including
metric/customary units, money, and temperature, but it is worth noting that the entire
measurement area, including topics that overlapped with those of the ACT, constituted only
14 percent of the KIRIS grade 12 mathematics assessment in 1994 (Kentucky Department of
Education, 1995b, p. 25).[3]

Two remaining content areas showed less overlap between the assessments.
Trigonometry is a relatively minor part (7 percent) of the ACT mathematics assessment, but
the specifications provide some detail, e.g., graphing trigonometric functions and solving
trigonometric equations (American College Testing, 1989, p. 9). In contrast, trigonometry is
listed with no elaboration as only one of 17 topics under the measurement category in the
KIRIS specifications (Kentucky Department of Education, 1993a, p. 19), and it has little
representation in the assessment. Conversely, data collection, representation, and
interpretation; and understanding simple statistics are listed as part of the pre-algebra
content area in the ACT specifications (American College Testing, 1989, p. 7), but
examination of two sample ACT assessments showed little representation of the types of data
analysis, probability, and statistics problems that are apparent in KIRIS. (In 1994, problems
in the data area constituted 14 percent of the KIRIS grade 12 mathematics assessment; see
Kentucky Department of Education, 1995b, p. 23).[4]

It is necessary to examine the assessments themselves as well as their frameworks to
judge their similarity. For this purpose, we compared two released ACT mathematics
assessments to two KIRIS mathematics assessments (the 1994 grade 12 and 1995 grade 11
assessments). As noted earlier, the ACT is entirely multiple choice and therefore does not
mirror some of the demands of KIRIS, such as the requirement in some KIRIS tasks that
students explain their answers. In terms of content, however, the two assessments showed
both similarities and differences.

An excerpt of roughly one-third of a released ACT assessment is shown in Figure 20.
One can see in this selection examples of some of the overlapping content areas noted above.
For example, several of the items on the first page would fall into the KIRIS number and
mathematical procedures categories, despite the lack of a similarly named category on the
ACT. There are also items representing other KIRIS topic areas, including algebraic
representations, functions, inequalities, similarity, trigonometry, coordinate systems, and
rate.

---

[3]The documentation shows four of 29 items reflecting measurement. However, because at least
two items appear to have been classified as being in two of the KIRIS content areas, the share
percentage of the assessment reflecting this content area may be a bit smaller than 14 percent.

[4]See previous footnote.

2 △ △ △ △ △ △ △ △ △ **2**

29. How many centimeters long is the diagonal of a rectangle that is 5 centimeters wide and 8 centimeters long, as shown below?

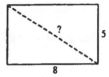

A. 13
B. $\sqrt{13}$
C. $\sqrt{40}$
D. $\sqrt{89}$
E. $\sqrt{99}$

32. The figure below shows 2 triangles, where $\triangle ABC \sim \triangle A'B'C'$. In these similar triangles, $a = 9$, $b = 12$, $c = 15$, and $a' = 15$, with all dimensions given in feet. What is the value of b'?

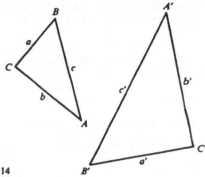

F. 14
G. 16
H. 18
J. 20
K. 22

30. Near a large city, planes take off from two airfields. One of the fields is capable of sending up a plane every 3 minutes. The other field is capable of sending up 2 planes every 7 minutes. At these rates, which of the following is the most reasonable estimate of the total number of planes the two airfields could send up in 90 minutes?

F. 18
G. 27
H. 36
J. 44
K. 55

33. In the (x,y) coordinate plane, if the point $(-4,2)$ is on the graph of $y = ax^2$, what is the value of a?

A. -1
B. 1
C. $-\frac{1}{2}$
D. $-\frac{1}{8}$
E. $\frac{1}{8}$

31. What are the (x,y) coordinates of the unique point on the graph of $x + 4y = 18$ such that the y-coordinate of that point is twice the x-coordinate?

A. (1,2)
B. (2,4)
C. (3,6)
D. (4,8)
E. (9,18)

34. The two parabolas $y = ax^2 + n$ and $y = x^2 + q$ have the same vertex when graphed in the (x,y) coordinate plane. Which of the following *must* be true?

F. $n + q = 0$
G. $nq = a$
H. $nq = 1$
J. $a = 1$
K. $n = q$

GO ON TO THE NEXT PAGE

Figure 20—Extract from ACT Mathematics Assessment

2 △ △ △ △ △ △ △ △ △ 2

MATHEMATICS TEST
60 Minutes—60 Questions

DIRECTIONS: Solve each problem, choose the correct answer, and then fill in the corresponding oval on your answer document.

Do not linger over problems that take too much time. Solve as many as you can; then return to the others in the time you have left for this test.

You are permitted to use a calculator on this test. You may use your calculator for any problems you choose, but some of the problems may best be done without using a calculator.

Note: Unless otherwise stated, all of the following should be assumed.

1. Illustrative figures are NOT necessarily drawn to scale.
2. Geometric figures lie in a plane.
3. The word *line* indicates a straight line.
4. The word *average* indicates arithmetic mean.

---

1. What is the average of 3, 3, and 4 ?

    A. 3
    B. $3\frac{1}{3}$
    C. $3\frac{1}{2}$
    D. $3\frac{2}{3}$
    E. 4

2. A positive number plus its square is equal to 56. What is the number?

    F. 5
    G. 6
    H. 7
    J. 8
    K. 9

3. For all x, $(2x - 3)(x + 5) = ?$

    A. $x^2 + 2x - 15$
    B. $2x^2 - 13x - 15$
    C. $2x^2 + 2x - 15$
    D. $2x^2 + 2x + 15$
    E. $2x^2 + 7x - 15$

4. A beaker of liquid cools from 19° to −6°. By how many degrees has it cooled?

    F. 6°
    G. 13°
    H. 19°
    J. 25°
    K. 26°

5. In the figure below, parallel lines r and s are intersected by line t. What is the measure of angle α ?

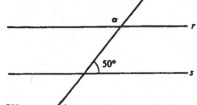

    A. 50°
    B. 100°
    C. 130°
    D. 140°
    E. 150°

6. Ticket sales for this year's annual concert at County Stadium were $350,000. The promoter is predicting that next year's ticket sales, in dollars, will be 60% greater than this year's. How many dollars in ticket sales is the promoter predicting for next year?

    F. $350,060
    G. $410,000
    H. $560,000
    J. $583,333
    K. $950,000

7. Adjacent segments in the hexagon below are perpendicular, and 4 segments are each 3 yards long, as marked. What is the perimeter of the hexagon, in yards?

    A. 12
    B. 18
    C. 24
    D. 27
    E. 30

ACT-53C

GO ON TO THE NEXT PAGE.

Figure 20 (continued)

2   **2**

51. In the figure below, what is the sine of $\angle BAC$?

A. $\frac{3}{5}$

B. $\frac{3}{4}$

C. $\frac{5}{3}$

D. $\frac{3}{\sqrt{34}}$

E. $\frac{5}{\sqrt{34}}$

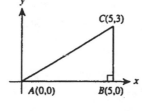

52. While watching TV from 7:00 P.M. to 8:00 P.M., you count 20 commercials, each 30 seconds long. To the nearest percent, what percent of the hour is taken up by commercials?

F. 6%
G. 10%
H. 17%
J. 50%
K. 60%

53. The sum of the 3 integers x, y, and z is 100. If $0 < x < 40$, and $y < 0$, what is the smallest possible value for z ?

A. 58
B. 59
C. 60
D. 61
E. 62

54. If $(x + m)^2 = x^2 + 12x + n$, where m and n are integers, what is the value of n ?

F. 36
G. 30
H. 24
J. 18
K. 12

55. What is the length, in coordinate units, of the diameter of a circle whose endpoints have coordinates (12,3) and (6,-5) in the standard (x,y) coordinate plane?

A. $\sqrt{28}$
B. $\sqrt{80}$
C. $\sqrt{82}$
D. $\sqrt{100}$
E. $\sqrt{202}$

56. The circle $(x - 1)^2 + (y - 2)^2 = 26$ intersects the y-axis in two points, one of which is (0,7). At what other point does the circle intersect the y-axis?

F. (0,-7)
G. (0,-3)
H. (0,3)
J. (0,$\sqrt{26}$)
K. (7,0)

57. If $x + y = 6$, then $x^2 = ?$

A. $y^2 - 12y - 36$
B. $y^2 - 36$
C. $6 - y^2$
D. $36 - y^2$
E. $36 - 12y + y^2$

58. Which of the following is the graph of the solution set for $x^2 < 9$?

F.
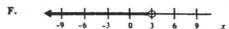

G.

H.
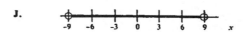

J.

K.
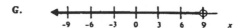

59. There is a pattern in the units digit of the positive integer powers of each whole number. Some powers of 2 are shown below. What is the units digit of 3^{45} ?

Powers of 2	Units digit
$2^1 = 2$	2
$2^2 = 4$	4
$2^3 = 8$	8
$2^4 = 16$	6
$2^5 = 32$	2
$2^6 = 64$	4
$2^7 = 128$	8
$2^8 = 256$	6

A. 1
B. 3
C. 5
D. 7
E. 9

THE NEXT PAGE

Figure 20 (continued)

This selection from the ACT can also be used to illustrate numerous differences between the two assessments. One important difference is that in terms of the content of a traditional mathematics course sequence for college-bound students, the ACT includes a greater amount of advanced content (which need not mean more difficult items) than does KIRIS. For example, KIRIS lacks the range of algebra content evident in the ACT. Figure 21 shows some KIRIS algebra items, which can be contrasted with those in Figure 20.

7. In art and in architecture, there are rectangles with proportions that make them most pleasing to the eye. In such "Golden Rectangles," the length and width satisfy the equation

$$\frac{L + W}{L} = \frac{L}{W}$$

a. Why is the equation above equivalent to $1 + \frac{W}{L} = \frac{L}{W}$?

b. Let x be the ratio of the length to the width (the golden ratio). Substitute into the equation in part a, and solve to find the approximate numerical value of the golden ratio (x). (Note: $\frac{L}{W} = x$)

Figure 21—KIRIS Grade 11 Mathematics Item 27, 1995

Conversely, consistent with differences in the assessments' frameworks, there is one content area in which KIRIS has markedly more coverage than the ACT: data analysis, probability, and statistics. In this area, KIRIS goes well beyond the now common tasks involving simple probabilities, such as the calculation of probabilities from random draws. All of the KIRIS items best suited to illustrating this material, however, remain secure, so they cannot be presented or described here.

Apart from format and formal content, many KIRIS items differ in other respects from those found in the ACT. For example, the high school KIRIS assessment, like the fourth-grade assessment described above for comparison to NAEP, has a substantial number of items requiring that students discern and sometimes extend a pattern. These items, which may entail mathematical series, geometric patterns, or other patterns, often have the flavor of puzzles. One example, this one involving geometric patterns, is shown in Figure 22. Another example, this one focusing on mathematical patterns, is shown in Figure 23. KIRIS also includes a smaller number of items that might be called spatial puzzles; an example is given in Figure 24.

8. Ms. Martine's class chose a pattern to be used on the classroom floor. The figure below illustrates the pattern they chose. The base pattern is a large square made up of 8 white and 8 shaded unit squares.

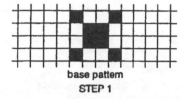

base pattern
STEP 1

Next, they expanded the pattern as pictured below.

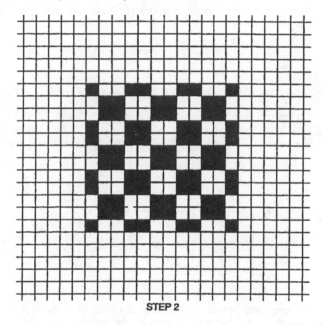

STEP 2

a. How many duplicates of the base pattern were **added** in order to complete STEP 2 of the pattern? How many shaded unit squares were **added** in STEP 2?

b. Each step is accomplished by surrounding the figure with copies of the base pattern. Expand the pattern by drawing STEP 3 on the grid provided in your Student Response Booklet. How many duplicates of the base pattern did you add to complete STEP 3? How many shaded unit squares were added?

c. Using the information from STEPS 1, 2, and 3, how many shaded unit squares will be added in STEP 6?

d. Write a generalization, or rule, for determining the number of shaded unit squares added in STEP **n**. Explain how you determined this generalization.

BE SURE TO LABEL YOUR RESPONSES (a), (b), (c) AND (d).

Figure 22—KIRIS Grade 11 Mathematics Item 10, 1995

8. a. Select three consecutive even integers.
   - Square the second number.
   - Multiply the first number by the third number.

   Repeat the process using two different sets of three consecutive even integers. What number pattern(s) did you observe?

   b. Select three integers that are every third integer in the set of integers, such as − 5, −2, 1.
   - Square the second number.
   - Multiply the first number by the third number.

   Repeat the process using two different sets of three integers that are every third integer in the set. What pattern(s) did you observe?

   c. Predict what pattern(s) will occur when you select three integers that are every *nth* integer in the set of integers. Mathematically justify your conclusion.

   BE SURE TO LABEL YOUR RESPONSES (a), (b), AND (c).

Figure 23—KIRIS Grade 11 Mathematics Item 7, 1995

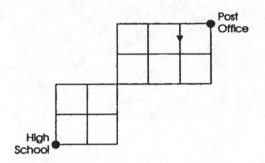

b. Above is a grid showing the streets connecting Danville High School to the Danville Post Office. The arrow on the grid indicates that for one block only that street is one-way in the direction of the arrow. How many routes can be traveled from Danville High School to the Danville Post Office if travel must always be to the right or up?

c. Using the diagram in part b, discuss the effect of having the one-way street on the total number of routes that can be traveled.

Figure 24—KIRIS Grade 11 Mathematics Item 33, 1994

ACT TRENDS, 1992-94: THE OEA ANALYSIS

The OEA Panel compared trends in scores on the ACT and KIRIS in reading and mathematics for twelfth-grade students who took both tests. To address the problem of the self-selection of students taking the ACT, the OEA Panel recomputed KIRIS trends for the subset of students who took the ACT and used the recomputed KIRIS trends as the basis for comparison with ACT trends. The KIRIS trends recomputed for students who took the ACT were quite similar to the KIRIS trends observed for the entire state, increasing the Panel's confidence in the utility of the comparison with ACT scores.[5]

The students who took the ACT showed substantial gains on KIRIS in both reading (0.26 standard deviation) and mathematics (0.36 standard deviation), but these gains were not reflected in their ACT scores. Their ACT scores showed essentially no change in either subject (Hambleton, et al., 1995, pp. 8-12 through 8-13).

The OEA Panel also examined changes in the consistency between ACT and KIRIS scores over the three-year period from 1992 through 1994, measured by the school-level correlation between scores on the two tests. The Panel found that these correlations dropped over time. In mathematics, for example, the correlation dropped from roughly 0.7 in 1992 and 1993 to approximately 0.5 in 1994. The Panel interpreted this change as suggesting that schools engaged in differing amounts of test preparation that did not produce gains in achievement that generalized to the ACT (Hambleton, et al., 1995, pp. 8-14 through 8-15).

Our analysis of more recent data also found a divergence in trends between the two assessments but did not confirm the decline in correlations between the ACT and KIRIS.

ACT TRENDS THROUGH 1995

Data linking ACT and KIRIS scores are not available till long after students take KIRIS in the eleventh grade, because many students do not take the ACT until their senior year or retake it at that time. When this report was written, merged data were only available through 1995. However, because KIRIS showed no aggregate gains in 1996 (see Figure 9), the lack of more recent data were deemed not important for our purposes.

The ACT assessment comprises four subtests: reading, mathematics, science reasoning, and English. We compared the first three of these to the KIRIS reading, mathematics, and science tests. The ACT English test is a 75-item multiple-choice test that measures "understanding of the conventions of standard written English (punctuation, and usage, and sentence structure) and of rhetorical skills (strategy, organization, and style)" (American College Testing, 1996). KIRIS includes no close analogue of this test, so it was not used in the comparisons presented here.

Mathematics trends are the most clear-cut, and they also show the most striking divergence between ACT and KIRIS scores. Between 1994 and 1995, the KIRIS gains for students taking the ACT continued at the rapid pace shown the year before. Over the three years, the mean KIRIS score increased by 0.7 standard deviation, a remarkably large gain, while ACT scores dropped very slightly, by 0.04 standard deviation (Figure 25).

---

[5]Because of data limitations, the OEA Panel also had to compute KIRIS scores using only common items in the transitional assessment—those open-response items administered to all students. This appears to have had little impact on the results.

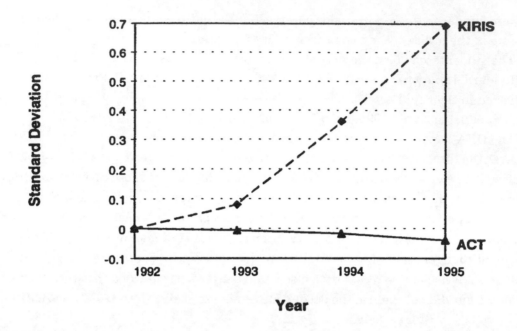

Figure 25—Standardized Changes in ACT and KIRIS Mathematics

KIRIS gains in reading also show no reflection in ACT scores, but the comparison is clouded by fluctuations in KIRIS scores. From 1992 to 1993, the mean KIRIS score in reading fell by almost 0.25 standard deviation (Figure 26). The following year, the mean score increased by roughly 0.5 standard deviation, which is an extraordinary change for a single year. The third year scores increased modestly, by 0.13 standard deviation. This large annual fluctuation casts doubt on the accuracy of annual change estimates in the first years of the program. Between 1992 and 1995, the average KIRIS score increased by 0.37 standard deviation, while ACT scores for the same students remained essentially constant (increasing by a trivial 0.02 standard deviation).

Science provides the least clear-cut comparison because it shows modest gains in ACT scores as well as a fluctuation in KIRIS means, but it too shows a marked discrepancy between KIRIS and ACT trends. KIRIS science scores dropped modestly in 1993 and then rose sharply in 1994 and 1995, producing a total cumulative gain from 1992 to 1995 of over 0.4 standard deviation (Figure 27). During this period, the mean ACT score in science obtained by the same students rose slowly but steadily, creating a cumulative gain of just under 0.1 standard deviation. This ACT gain of about 0.1 standard deviation indicates that the median ACT-taker in Kentucky in 1995 (the student at the 50th percentile) scored at roughly the same level on the ACT as the student at the 54th percentile in 1992. On KIRIS, the median ACT-taker in 1995 scored at the same level as the student at the 67th percentile in 1992.

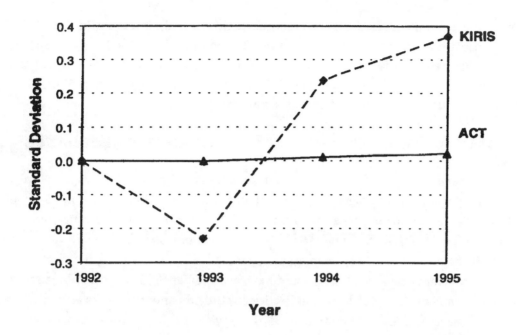

Figure 26—Standardized Changes in ACT and KIRIS Reading

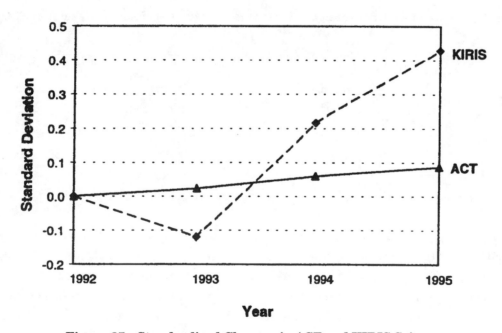

Figure 27—Standardized Changes in ACT and KIRIS Science

Thus, KIRIS science gains were accompanied by ACT gains roughly one-fifth as large. While this may suggest that KIRIS gains overstate improvements in student learning, it is important to note that the modest increase on the ACT would be large if continued over the long term. For example, over the 20-year accountability period envisioned in the KERA program, a continuing increase of the magnitude shown by ACT scores during these three years would raise the median student to a level comparable to the 73rd percentile at the outset of the program. Whether this echo of KIRIS gains in ACT scores is attributable to KERA cannot be determined from these data, however.

CHANGES IN ACT SCORES OF STUDENTS AT THE KIRIS PERFORMANCE LEVELS

The disparity between KIRIS and ACT trends was not limited to averages. It also appeared as a drop in the average ACT scores of students at all KIRIS performance levels.

In mathematics, the average ACT scores of students scoring at the Proficient or Distinguished levels on KIRIS dropped by half a standard deviation in the two years from 1993 to 1995 (Table 14).[6] If these changes are translated into percentiles, they indicate that the median Proficient student in 1995 would have obtained an ACT score similar to that of the student at the 30th percentile among Proficient students only two years earlier. The declines in average ACT scores for students at the Novice and Apprentice levels were somewhat smaller but were nonetheless sizable, particularly for such a short time.

Table 14

Change in Mean ACT Scores of Students at Each KIRIS Performance Level, 1993-95, by Subject

	Mathematics		Reading		Science	
	Raw Change	Standardized Change[a]	Raw Change	Standardized Change[a]	Raw Change	Standardized Change[a]
Novice	−1.5	−0.33	−1.7	−0.29	−1.3	−0.29
Apprentice	−1.8	−0.40	−1.4	−0.24	−0.7	−0.16
Proficient	−2.3	−0.51	−0.9	−0.15	−1.5	−0.35
Distinguished	−2.3	−0.51	−1.5	−0.25	−2.1	−0.48

[a]Changes were standardized using the 1994 standard deviation of ACT scores in our analysis sample.

In reading and science as well, the divergence between ACT and KIRIS trends was apparent at all KIRIS performance levels, but the rank ordering of the changes differed across subjects. The changes in reading were all smaller than those in mathematics (as one would expect from the smaller changes in mean scores noted above), and the size of the change was comparable at all performance levels other than Proficient (Table 14). In science, as in mathematics, the largest decline in ACT scores was for students at the Distinguished level.

These declines in ACT scores reflect the movement of students into higher KIRIS levels as KIRIS scores increased and ACT scores either remained essentially unchanged (in mathematics and reading) or increased much more modestly (in science). For example, in

---

[6]Scores for 1992 are not considered here, because the 1992 KIRIS performance levels cannot be precisely linked to those used in later years.

1993, 43 percent of ACT-takers were classified as Novice in mathematics, compared to only 17 percent two years later. At the same time, the percentage of ACT-takers classified as Proficient increased from 13 percent to 25 percent, and those classified as Distinguished doubled from 8 percent to 16 percent. The effect of these changes was to leave behind in the Novice category a shrinking pool of ever lower-scoring students, while students moving into the higher performance levels scored on average less well on the ACT than the students who had been in those categories in previous years.

CORRELATIONS BETWEEN ACT AND KIRIS SCORES

Correlations between scores on the ACT and KIRIS assessments are important for several reasons. Moderate to large cross-sectional correlations between the tests suggest overlap in the constructs they measure and therefore support the appropriateness of comparing trends on the two assessments as part of an effort to evaluate KIRIS gains. Second, such correlations might also be seen as cross-sectional evidence supporting the validity of KIRIS. Finally, changes in these correlations over time might bear on the validity of KIRIS gains. For example, as noted in the OEA Panel report, a decline in the correlation between ACT and KIRIS scores over time would indicate that gains in KIRIS were reflected in ACT scores less in some schools than in others. When accompanied by a lack of gains in ACT scores, this might suggest that differences in test preparation or other factors led to greater inflation of KIRIS gains in some schools than in others.

Student-level correlations between KIRIS NAPD scores and ACT scores were moderate in reading and science—a bit under 0.50 (Table 15). They were higher in mathematics, generally around 0.70. These student-level correlations are more substantial than they appear; they are attenuated by measurement error, particularly in KIRIS (which is not designed to produce reliable student-level scores), and they are bounded at less than 1.0 because the NAPD scores are discrete. In no case did the correlations erode over time; the only substantial change was the increase in the correlation in mathematics after 1992.

Table 15

Student-Level Correlations Between ACT and KIRIS Scores

	1992	1993	1994	1995
Reading	0.47	0.45	0.46	0.46
Mathematics	0.54	0.71	0.70	0.72
Science	0.41	0.45	0.48	0.46

NOTE: The 1992 correlations reflect the old scoring system; other years reflect the new scoring system. The impact of this change on these correlations was minor.

School-level correlations between ACT and KIRIS scores (that is, the correlations between school means on the two tests) were moderate to high in all three subjects. With the exception of 1994, the correlations were roughly 0.6 in reading and science and 0.7 in mathematics (Table 16). These correlations are attenuated to some degree by sampling error because of the small number of students in some schools who took both tests. As noted by the OEA Panel, these correlations dipped substantially in reading and mathematics in 1994; they also dropped, but less, in science (which the OEA Panel did not examine). This dip was temporary, however, and in all three subjects, the correlation in 1995 was as high as or higher than the correlation in 1992.

Table 16

School-Level Correlations Between ACT and KIRIS Scores

	1992	1993	1994	1995
Reading	0.59	0.58	0.36	0.59
Mathematics	0.69	0.75	0.58	0.74
Science	0.58	0.58	0.51	0.66

NOTE: The 1992 correlations reflect the old scoring system; other years reflect the new scoring system. The impact of this change on these correlations was minor.

In sum, then, student- and school-level correlations between ACT and KIRIS scores were moderate to high and stayed reasonably consistent over the 1992-95 period. As KDE has argued, these findings can be seen as cross-sectional evidence of the validity of KIRIS, and they do not offer a reason to question the validity of KIRIS gains over time.

VARIATIONS AMONG SCHOOLS IN THE DISCREPANCY BETWEEN ACT AND KIRIS TRENDS

Although the school-level correlations between ACT and KIRIS mean scores remained quite stable, the divergence between ACT and KIRIS trends varied among schools. This variation was explored using mathematics scores, which showed the greatest divergence between KIRIS and ACT trends.

To facilitate comparisons between the two assessments, ACT scores were projected onto the KIRIS scale.[7] Once the ACT was placed on the KIRIS scale, virtually all schools— all but three of the 224 schools included in this analysis—had larger gains on KIRIS than on the ACT. These schools are above the lower, solid line in Figure 28, which represents equal change on the two tests. Most schools showed much larger gains on KIRIS, although there was a great deal of variation among schools in this respect. The average discrepancy in gain was 26 points on the KIRIS scale (the median was 25 points), and the maximum was 55 points.

---

[7]This was done by regressing 1993 KIRIS mean scores on mean ACT scores and the percentage of students in a school taking the ACT. (The latter variable was included as a control for differences in the selectivity of the groups taking the ACT.) The predicted values from this equation were adjusted by inflating their variance to match the variance of observed KIRIS scores. These adjusted values were used to place 1993 ACT school means on the KIRIS scale. ACT means for 1995 were projected onto the KIRIS scale by substituting the 1995 values of both the ACT and the percentage of students taking the ACT into the 1993 equation and again inflating the variance to match the observed KIRIS variance in 1993.

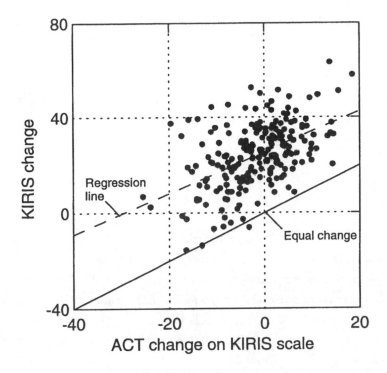

**Figure 28—Change in School Mean KIRIS Math Scores vs.
Change in Mean ACT Math Scores on the KIRIS Scale,
1993-95**

To some degree, change on KIRIS was predictable from change on the ACT. A simple regression of KIRIS change on ACT change is shown by the upper, dashed line in Figure 28. The regression line (with a slope of 0.9) is nearly parallel to the line indicating equal change, only about 26 points higher. In other words, on average, zero change on the ACT leads to a prediction of a 26-point gain on KIRIS, and every additional one point of gain on the ACT (on the KIRIS scale) predicts an additional increase in KIRIS gains of about 0.9 point. The scatter around the regression line is substantial, however, indicating that most schools vary considerably from this prediction. The R^2 is about 0.25, indicating that about 25 percent of the variability in KIRIS gains—but not the mean difference in gains between the assessments—can be predicted from changes in ACT scores.

The few variables considered here reveal few differences between schools whose KIRIS gains were markedly more and markedly less than predicted. Schools were broken into quartiles based on the discrepancy between their actual and predicted gains on KIRIS, and three groups—the top quartile, the bottom quartile, and the middle two quartiles together— were compared. These three groups had nearly identical mean ACT scores and similar percentages of students taking the ACT at the start of the trend in 1993. None of the three groups of schools showed an appreciable change in ACT scores from 1993 to 1995. They differed slightly in initial (1993) KIRIS means (41 for the bottom quartile, 37 for the middle two quartiles, and 34 for the top quartile), but this small negative relationship between initial scores and gain is probably an artifact of regression to the mean. Thus, the schools showing more gain on KIRIS than predicted differed substantially from those with less gain than predicted in terms of only one of the variables considered here: final (1995) KIRIS scores. Schools with large (positive) discrepancies between KIRIS and ACT changes tended to be those with high KIRIS scores in 1995 and therefore with unusually large KIRIS gains. The bottom quartile group, with KIRIS gains much smaller than predicted from ACT scores, had a KIRIS mean of 50 in 1995; the middle half had a mean of 61; and the high-gain quartile had a mean of 73.

In sum, schools' gains on KIRIS were usually larger than their gains on the ACT (once the latter were put on the KIRIS scale), in most cases by a large margin. The causes of this discrepancy were clearly widespread, as almost all schools showed a positive discrepancy between KIRIS change and ACT change. Apart from this mean difference, the amount of change schools showed on the ACT predicted about one-fourth of the variability of gains on KIRIS. This indicates the extent to which change on the two tests represents common influences. One set of common influences could be instructional changes that influence scores on both tests. Another is cohort differences. That is, one of the major sources of error in estimating school performance is that schools may have "good" and "bad" cohorts in different years, causing their scores to fluctuate even if instruction is equally effective in every year.

Three-fourths of the variability in gain on KIRIS, however, could not be predicted from change on the ACT. These variations could not be explained in terms of initial ACT scores, initial KIRIS scores, or selectivity (percentage of students taking the ACT). They could reflect instructional changes or cohort differences reflected more in one test than in the other, inflated gains from inappropriate teaching to the test, or sources of error other than sampling of students.

9. INTERNAL EVIDENCE FROM KIRIS DATA THROUGH 1995

Data internal to a single assessment are often used to provide validity evidence. Such data have been used numerous times to evaluate KIRIS, although not to evaluate gains in scores. For example, the OEA Panel and KDE both used internal convergent-discriminant evidence in their efforts to evaluate the validity of cross-sectional inferences based on KIRIS. That is, they investigated whether components of the assessment that purport to measure related constructs show stronger empirical relationships with each other than do parts of the assessment that purport to measure less related constructs. Similarly, Koretz (1997) used a variety of internal measures, such as analysis of differential item functioning and item discrimination, to evaluate the validity of inferences about the performance of Kentucky students with disabilities based on their KIRIS scores. Internal analysis can also provide evidence pertaining to the validity of gains on KIRIS, but it had not been used for that purpose prior to our study.

The primary opportunity for using internal evidence to address the validity of gains stems from the reuse of KIRIS items over time. A given KIRIS assessment consists largely of items that have been used in previous years. After each assessment, a number of items that will no longer be used are publicly released and may be used in instruction. Other items are kept secure for future use. The following year, new items are introduced to replace those that were released in the previous year. Therefore, if the true relative difficulty of new and reused items were clearly established, differences in performance on new and reused items could shed light on the validity of gains. If performance on new and reused items were similar after true differences in difficulty were accounted for, that would be positive evidence for validity, because it would suggest that teachers were not tailoring their instruction and test preparation too narrowly to the content of reused items. Conversely, if performance were substantially lower on new items after true difficulty differences were taken into account, that might indicate inflation of gains. For example, it might reflect either coaching on previously used but still secure items, which KDE explicitly prohibits, or coaching that is overly narrowly focused on the specific content or task demands of the reused items rather than on the domains of knowledge and skill they are intended to represent.

Unfortunately, KIRIS does not provide clear information about the relative difficulty of new and reused items. The method used to equate KIRIS across years does not provide that information; rather, the method is based on the assumption that the difficulty of items remains constant when they are reused. In other words, the equating method used with KIRIS simply assumes that some of the factors that could undermine the validity of gains— such as inappropriate coaching tailored to reused items—do not arise. Other equating methods, such as the administration of new and reused items to samples of out-of-state students who have had no previous experience with the assessment, in theory could provide information on relative difficulty. That approach faces other obstacles, however, and has not been used with the transitional assessments. One reason is that the novelty of some KIRIS tasks might make the performance of many out-of-state students so low as to be useless for this purpose.

As a result, observed differences in performance on new and reused KIRIS items are difficult to interpret. Better performance on reused items might represent true differences in difficulty, the effects of coaching and practice, or both.

Accordingly, we used several approaches jointly in an attempt to circumvent the lack of clear information about the relative difficulty of new and reused items. All were applied to mathematics and reading in grades 4 and 8.

METHODS USED IN INTERNAL ANALYSIS

One of our approaches to the internal analysis of KIRIS performance was to simply compare the observed performance levels on new and reused items. The difference in performance between new and reused items is referred to as a "discrepancy measure." In theory, new items each year are random draws from the same domains of content and skills represented by previously used items. While a given new item might be easier or harder than a given reused item, such random variation would not make new items consistently or systematically more difficult, and discrepancy measures therefore ought to vary randomly in direction and size. Accordingly, erratic differences in difficulty between new and reused items would be encouraging, while consistently lower performance on new items relative to reused items might suggest inflated scores. On the other hand, it is possible that there have been true, systematic differences in difficulty over time; for example, it is possible that new items really have been on average more difficult than reused ones. Because KIRIS does not provide firm information on relative difficulty, this possibility cannot be ruled out, and even systematic differences in performance on new and reused items would be at most suggestive and would point to the need for further evidence.

Our second approach was to examine performance on items as a function of their age. That is, we explored whether performance became progressively higher as an item was reused repeatedly. When test scores are rising, an improvement in performance over time on reused items would be expected and would not in itself be cause for concern. Such increases could represent either real improvements in learning or inflation of gains. However, trends in performance on individual items provide some context for interpreting differences in performance on new and reused items within an assessment year. Unlike differences on new and reused items within years, differences on the same items across years are not confounded by variations in the true difficulty of items written in different years. A consistent increase in performance as items become older, coupled with systematically lower performance on new items, might suggest the possibility of inflation. Moreover, analysis of performance changes over time can identify types of items that showed unusually large or small gains, and this in turn may hold clues about the validity of score increases.

Our third approach involved looking at *variations* in the discrepancy in performance on new and reused items. This approach assumes that the overall discrepancy in performance cannot be interpreted because the true difference in difficulty is unknown. However, the relationships between the size of the discrepancy measure and other variables could be informative. In particular, if the discrepancy tends to be larger (that is, if it favors reused items particularly strongly) in schools that showed relatively large gains in KIRIS scores, that might suggest coaching tailored to reused items and correspondingly inflated scores in high-gain schools. A finding of no association between KIRIS gains and discrepancy measures, however, would be harder to interpret. It would suggest that coaching of this sort played little role in the *relative* gains of schools, but it would say less about the overall impact of this form of coaching and nothing about other forms of coaching, e.g., those focused more generally on the content and format of the test.

Creating Item Sets

The first step required for these analyses was to place test items into sets on the basis of their use. This required us to create a complete mapping of all open-response items used in mathematics and reading in grades 4 and 8 in the assessments of 1992 through 1995, tracing the years in which each was used and the forms and positions in which they appeared.

Several partial maps of item placement and usage were available from KDE. These maps showed the placements in the assessments of most items that had been used in more than one year. The KDE maps excluded items that were not linked for purposes of equating the assessments from year to year, except for reused items that were changed from matrix to common. Items not documented in the KDE maps were items used only once, items that were new at the time a given map was created, and items that had been edited enough to be treated as new items for purposes of equating. Items that were edited in ways considered minor by Advanced Systems for Measurement in Education were linked for equating purposes and were included in the maps.

We augmented these maps by process of elimination. For example, all items in a given year that did not appear on the maps were assumed to be new (or edited enough to be considered new) and were added to the maps as new items. KIRIS items are generally grouped by subject (e.g., all mathematics items on a form appear in one subsection of a form), and the KDE maps identified items by placement rather than actual content. Advanced Systems for Measurement in Education had in some years placed some items in the midst of items from other subject areas in an effort to balance reading demands, and those items were therefore misclassified in terms of content in the KDE maps. We located and checked all such items and reclassified them as necessary. The maps were checked and corrected by examining all hard-copy assessment booklets for these subjects and grades for all years. Unique ID numbers for the items, a set of flags indicating the years in which items had been used, and an indicator showing whether items had been used as common or matrix items in each year were then added to these maps.

Even with this checking, some ambiguities and possible errors remained in the maps. For example, in theory, any item that was reused and converted from matrix to common was treated as a new item because of the risk that the change in position (common items come first in the booklet) would cause an artifactual increase in performance. In practice, Advanced Systems for Measurement in Education did use some of these items in equating (see, for example, Kentucky Department of Education, 1997, Table 9-4), but we were unable to ascertain which items these were. We also encountered uncertainties about the use of some other items; for example, it appears that some matrix items were not used in equating, but we were unable to identify all of them with confidence. KDE assisted us in eliminating some of these uncertainties, but some remained.

Items were then placed into sets to reflect their use based on these amended maps. Sets were defined first in terms of the newness of items in a given year. Set 1 for each subject, grade, and year comprised items that were used for the first time in that assessment. Set 2 consisted of items used in that year and the previous year, but not earlier. Set 3 comprised items used in that year and at least the two previous years. (This set could not be created for the 1993 assessment, because 1992 was the first administration of KIRIS.) A fourth set of all reused items was created by combining set 2 and set 3 for each assessment year.

Items were placed in only a single set for an assessment year, but most fell into additional sets for other years. For example, all items in set 2 for 1995 (those that were used for the second time in 1995) were necessarily in set 1 for 1994 (those that were used for the first time in 1994).

Accounting for Items That Became Common

Most items that were changed from matrix to common were not linked for purposes of equating and therefore did not contribute directly to gains in KIRIS scores. However, as noted above, some unidentified items of this sort were in practice used in equating and thus did contribute to score changes. Moreover, even items that were not used in equating could contribute to the *relative* gains of some schools and could shed light on score increases indirectly. While some portion of the performance gains on items that were made common might reflect changes in position, it is likely that some of the improvement also stemmed from teaching or coaching. Thus, examination of the items that showed particularly large gains in performance might help clarify the underpinnings of performance gains even when those items did not contribute directly to statewide score increases.

Accordingly, two variants of each set were created. One included all relevant items in the map. The second set, identified below as "matrix only," excluded all items that were made common in the last year relevant to a set. Where appropriate, analyses were replicated with both sets.

Creating Set Means

Several mean scores were created for each of these sets by taking the average across students for each item and then averaging across items:

- Means for comparisons within assessment years. For example, how did the 1995 mean of new items compare to the 1995 mean on items used for the second time? This would compare the 1995 means for sets 1 and 2 defined for that year.

- Means for comparisons across assessment years. For example, how did the 1995 mean of items used for the second time compare to the mean for those same items the previous year? This would use only a single set of items—set 2 as defined for 1995—but would use scores on those items in both 1995 and 1994.
- Rescored 1994 and 1995 means to make data from those years comparable to data from 1992 and 1993.

These rescored means were necessitated by a change in the scoring of KIRIS items in 1994. In the first two years of the assessment, items were scored on a four-point scale (1 through 4), and both off-topic and minimal responses were assigned a score of 1. Starting in the spring of 1994, however, items were scored on a five-point scale (0 through 4); off-topic responses received a score of 0, and only on-topic but minimal responses were given a score of 1 (Kentucky Department of Education, 1995b, p. 124). This change caused a sharp drop in mean scores on many items in 1994. Accordingly, for use in all comparisons involving 1993 results, all 1994 and 1995 means were recalculated after recoding each item as it would have been scored in 1993. These recoded values were used only where necessary, however, because their coarser scale lost information relative to the scale used in 1994 and 1995.

Most of the sets constructed for these analyses included few items, particularly when only matrix items were considered. To illustrate, Table 17 shows the counts of items for grade 4 mathematics and reading in the 1995 assessment. These small numbers require that one interpret the findings cautiously. In particular, little confidence should be placed in any single difference between item sets, such as the difference between reused and new items in a single subject, grade, and year. Instead, one should focus on patterns that are evident across a number of item sets.

Table 17

Number of Open-Response Items in Each Set, KIRIS Grade 4 Mathematics and Reading, 1995

	Set 1 (new)	Set 2 (used twice)	Set 3 (used more than twice)
All items			
Mathematics	14	9	6
Reading	13	12	4
Matrix only			
Mathematics	13	7	4
Reading	13	9	2

PERFORMANCE DIFFERENCES ON NEW AND REUSED ITEMS WITHIN ASSESSMENT YEARS

As expected, the relative difficulty of new and reused items varied considerably. In cases in which there was a sizable difference in average difficulty, however, new items were on average harder than reused ones.

To put these findings into perspective, it is necessary to recall the timing of the gains in mathematics and reading in grades 4 and 8. Fourth-grade mathematics showed a large gain in the first year and very large gains thereafter; fourth-grade reading showed very large gains in every year through 1995 (see Figure 8). Eighth-grade mathematics showed large gains in the first two years and a very large gain in the third (see Figure 10). In contrast, eighth-grade reading showed a large gain in the first year, a very large gain in the second year, but a slight *decline* in 1995. Thus, trends in overall scores do not suggest any difference in item difficulty in eighth-grade reading in 1995, which is consistent with the results shown below.

Tables 18 and 19 show our mean score results for grade 4.[1] In mathematics, despite large gains in mean scores, new items were on average only slightly more difficult than reused ones (Table 18). Moreover, the differences in performance on reused and new items (set 4 scores minus set 1 scores) became smaller yet when only matrix items were considered (bottom panel of Table 18). In fourth-grade reading, the average scores obtained on new and reused items were similar in the 1993 and 1995 assessments despite very large increases in mean scores, but scores on new items were markedly lower than those on reused items in 1994 (Table 19).

Table 18

Mean Scores on Items by Set, 1993-95, KIRIS Grade 4 Mathematics, All Items and Matrix Items Only

	Set 1 (new)	Set 2 (used twice)	Set 3 (used more than twice)	Set 4 (all reused)	Set 4- Set 1	Gain in mean KIRIS scores
All Items						
1993	1.59	1.67		1.67	0.08	0.18
1994	1.45	1.56	1.59	1.57	0.12	0.32
1995	1.58	1.63	1.69	1.64	0.06	0.20
Matrix Only						
1993	1.59	1.65		1.65	0.06	0.18
1994	1.45	1.54	0.95	1.48	0.03	0.32
1995	1.56	1.56	1.59	1.57	0.01	0.20

NOTE: "Large" gains are between 0.1 and 0.2 standard deviation; "very large" gains are equal to or greater than 0.2 standard deviation. Means for all 1993 sets are higher than they would be if items had been scored using the scale used in 1994 and 1995. Differences may include rounding error.

---

[1]In these two tables and Tables 20 and 21, overall statewide gains in mean KIRIS scores for the years in question are entered in the final column to provide a context for the item-level results.

Table 19

Mean Scores on Items by Set, 1993-95, KIRIS Grade 4 Reading, All Items and Matrix Items Only

	Set 1 (new)	Set 2 (used twice)	Set 3 (used more than twice)	Set 4 (all reused)	Set 4- Set 1	Gain in mean KIRIS scores
All Items						
1993	1.66	1.68		1.68	0.02	0.48
1994	1.54	1.83	1.81	1.82	0.28	0.28
1995	1.97	1.87	2.26	1.97	0.00	0.58
Matrix Only						
1993	1.66	1.64		1.64	-0.02	0.48
1994	1.54	1.79	1.77	1.78	0.24	0.28
1995	1.97	1.85	2.17	1.91	-0.06	0.58

NOTE: "Large" gains are between 0.1 and 0.2 standard deviation; "very large" gains are equal to or greater than 0.2 standard deviation. Means for all 1993 sets are higher than they would be if items had been scored using the scale used in 1994 and 1995. Differences may include rounding error.

Tables 20 and 21 show the results for grade 8. Here, in contrast to the grade 4 results, the average differences in performance on new and reused items are more substantial. In mathematics, the difference between new items and all reused items (set 4) was appreciable in all three years (Table 20). Omitting common items eliminated this difference in 1993 but left appreciable differences in 1994 and 1995 (lower panel, Table 20). In reading, because of the lack of statewide gains in 1995, only the 1993 and 1994 comparisons are germane. Reused and new items were similar in difficulty in 1993, but new items were markedly more difficult in 1994 (Table 21).

Table 20

Mean Scores on Items by Set, 1993-95, KIRIS Grade 8 Mathematics, All Items and Matrix Items Only

	Set 1 (new)	Set 2 (used twice)	Set 3 (used more than twice)	Set 4 (all reused)	Set 4- Set 1	Gain in mean KIRIS scores
All Items						
1993	1.47	1.68		1.68	0.21	0.12
1994	0.76	1.25	1.31	1.27	0.51	0.18
1995	1.07	1.33	1.45	1.42	0.35	0.26
Matrix Only						
1993	1.48	1.49		1.49	-0.01	0.12
1994	0.76	1.18	1.26	1.20	0.44	0.18
1995	1.08	1.17	1.29	1.27	0.19	0.26

NOTE: "Large" gains are between 0.1 and 0.2 standard deviation; "very large" gains are equal to or greater than 0.2 standard deviation. Means for all 1993 sets are higher than they would be if items had been scored using the scale used in 1994 and 1995. Differences may include rounding error.

Table 21

Mean Scores on Items by Set, 1993-95, KIRIS Grade 8 Reading, All Items and Matrix Items Only

	Set 1 (new)	Set 2 (used twice)	Set 3 (used more than twice)	Set 4 (all reused)	Set 4- Set 1	Gain in mean KIRIS scores
All Items						
1993	1.75	1.76		1.76	0.01	0.12
1994	1.78	1.96	2.08	2.00	0.22	0.28
1995	1.89	1.91	1.92	1.91	0.02	-0.04
Matrix Only						
1993	1.75	1.77		1.77	0.02	0.12
1994	1.78	1.87	2.05	1.92	0.14	0.28
1995	1.85	1.86	1.91	1.89	0.04	-0.04

NOTE: "Large" gains are between 0.1 and 0.2 standard deviation; "very large" gains are equal to or greater than 0.2 standard deviation. Means for all 1993 sets are higher than they would be if items had been scored using the scale used in 1994 and 1995. Differences may include rounding error.

Although these differences appear small relative to the full range of possible scores (0 through 4), the larger of them are substantial relative to the actual variation in scores. In other words, most of the variation in performance occurs within a small portion of the scale, so even a difference of a fraction of a scale point can be large in comparison. In the case of these mean differences on individual items, a reasonable standard of comparison is the total variability of item means. We used the variability of new items as a standard of comparison because there had been no opportunity to coach students on these items. Because the items within sets are so few, this variability is shown better by examination of the entire distribution of item means than by a summary statistic such as a standard deviation.

The size of the larger mean differences is illustrated by the performance differences on reused and new eighth-grade mathematics items in 1994 and 1995: 0.51 and 0.35, respectively, on the 0-4 scale (Table 20). Consider first the 1995 mean difference of 0.35. In 1995, 15 new mathematics items were used; the total range of their means was about 0.9. (See Figure 29, in which the mean for each new item is represented by a point, and the size of the performance difference on new and reused items is approximated by the length of the vertical bar to the left of each distribution.) Ten of the 15 items had means within a range of 0.5 point, and half of the new items had means within a range of approximately 0.35 point, comparable to the mean difference in performance on new and reused items in that year.

The pattern in 1994 was less clear-cut. Although the mean performance difference on new and reused items was larger than in 1995, the fewer (seven) new mathematics items in 1994 showed more variable performance than those in 1995. The total range of new item means was 1.3 points, but five of the seven (either the five highest or the five lowest) fell within a range of roughly 0.9 point. By contrast, the mean performance difference on new and reused items was 0.51 point (left-hand vertical line in Figure 29).

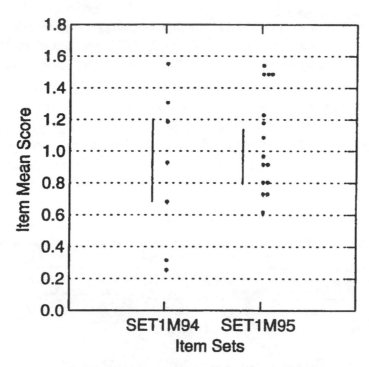

NOTE: Each point is the mean on one item. Vertical bars represent the mean difference between new and reused items.

Figure 29—Mean Scores on New Mathematics Items, KIRIS
Grade 8, 1994 and 1995

In sum, these differences in performance on new and reused items provide only weak and inconsistent evidence of coaching that might undermine the validity of gains. The general pattern—performance that is sometimes appreciably lower on new items and is never substantially higher—is consistent with coaching, and there were instances in grade 8 in which the differences are large. On the other hand, there were no substantial differences in item difficulty in numerous cases, particularly in grade 4. As noted earlier, however, in the absence of clear information about the relative difficulty of new and reused items, these differences (or the lack of differences) by themselves are not sufficient evidence; rather, they must be taken together with other forms of evidence, described below.

CHANGES IN PERFORMANCE ON REUSED ITEMS ACROSS YEARS

Taken by itself, an increase in performance on reused items when average scores are rising is not informative. As noted earlier, when scores are rising, performance on reused items will generally improve, and that improvement in and of itself does not indicate whether the gains in scores are valid indicators of improved learning. These trends, however, provide a context for understanding performance differences on new and reused items. In particular, there may be grounds for concern if a plot of item difficulty over time shows a "sawtooth" pattern: a consistent pattern in which performance on items goes up as they are reused, but these performance gains are not echoed in new items as they are introduced.

In grade 4, performance on reused mathematics items grew progressively better over time, and many of the increases in scores were sizable. With one exception, the changes were similar for matrix items only and for all items. For example, performance on 1995 set 2 mathematics items—those used for the second time in 1995—increased by 0.20 point from 1994 to 1995 (Table 22). Performance on all 1995 set 3 mathematics items increased by nearly 0.6 point over the two-year period from 1993 to 1995, while scores on set 3 matrix items increased by nearly 0.5 point during that period. The one-year increases are moderate in size relative to the variation in means on new items. In 1995, for example, all but three of the 14 new mathematics items had mean scores within a range of 0.4 point.

Table 22

Changes in Mean Item Performance Across Years, KIRIS Grade 4 Mathematics, All Items and Matrix Items Only

	Means			Differences		
	1993[a]	1994	1995	1994-1993	1995-1994	Counts
All Items						
Set 2 1995		1.43	1.63		0.20	9
Set 3 1995	1.12	1.40	1.69	0.28	0.29	6
Set 2 1994	1.37	1.56		0.19		12
Matrix Items Only						
Set 2 1995		1.36	1.56		0.20	7
Set 3 1995	1.13	1.42	1.59	0.29	0.17	4
Set 2 1994	1.33	1.54		0.21		9

[a]The 1993 means are estimates of values on the new (1994) scale obtained by subtracting from the 1994 values on the new scale the difference between 1994 and 1993 means on the old scale.

Fourth-grade reading items also showed increases in performance over time (Table 23). For example, the mean score on all 1995 set 3 reading items increased by almost 0.6 point from 1993 to 1995, while set 3 matrix items showed an increase of about 0.4 point over those two years. By way of comparison, eight of the 13 new items in 1995 were within a range of 0.4 point.

Increases in performance on reused mathematics items were generally smaller in grade 8 than in grade 4 from 1993 to 1994 (Table 24). From 1994 to 1995, however, the increases in scores in eighth grade were larger and were quite similar to those in the fourth grade.

In the eighth grade, reused reading items showed modest increases in performance from 1993 to 1994 (Table 25). The increases in performance from 1994 to 1995 were small, but that is not surprising given that mean KIRIS scores in eighth-grade reading did not increase in 1995.

Table 23

Changes in Mean Item Performance Across Years, KIRIS Grade 4 Reading, All Items and Matrix Items Only

	Means			Differences		
	1993[a]	1994	1995	1994-1993	1995-1994	Counts
All Items						
Set 2 1995		1.55	1.87		0.32	12
Set 3 1995	1.69	1.85	2.26	0.16	0.41	4
Set 2 1994	1.64	1.83		0.19		9
Matrix Items Only						
Set 2 1995		1.58	1.85		0.27	9
Set 3 1995	1.75	1.92	2.17	0.17	0.25	2
Set 2 1994	1.64	1.79		0.15		5

[a]The 1993 means are estimates of values on the new (1994) scale obtained by subtracting from the 1994 values on the new scale the difference between 1994 and 1993 means on the old scale.

Table 24

Changes in Mean Item Performance Across Years, KIRIS Grade 8 Mathematics, All Items and Matrix Items Only

	Means			Differences		
	1993[a]	1994	1995	1994-1993	1995-1994	Counts
All Items						
Set 2 1995		1.02	1.33		0.31	4
Set 3 1995	1.12	1.21	1.45	0.09	0.24	11
Set 2 1994	1.18	1.25		0.07		15
Matrix Items Only						
Set 2 1995		1.06	1.17		0.11	2
Set 3 1995	0.97	1.08	1.29	0.11	0.21	8
Set 2 1994	1.14	1.18		0.04		13

[a]The 1993 means are estimates of values on the new (1994) scale obtained by subtracting from the 1994 values on the new scale the difference between 1994 and 1993 means on the old scale.

In sum, in most instances other than the one in which performance increases were not expected (grade 8 reading in 1995), performance on reused items increased over time. The rate of annual increase was typically moderate relative to the variation in performance on new items.

Table 25

Changes in Mean Item Performance Across Years, KIRIS Grade 8 Reading, All Items and Matrix Items Only

	Means			Differences		
	1993[a]	1994	1995	1994-1993	1995-1994	Counts
All Items						
Set 2 1995		1.81	1.91		0.10	6
Set 3 1995	1.75	1.87	1.92	0.12	0.05	10
Set 2 1994	1.76	1.96		0.20		12
Reading						
Set 2 1995		1.75	1.86		0.11	4
Set 3 1995	1.73	1.87	1.91	0.14	0.04	7
Set 2 1994	1.74	1.87		0.13		9

[a]The 1993 means are estimates of values on the new (1994) scale obtained by subtracting from the 1994 values on the new scale the difference between 1994 and 1993 means on the old scale.

THE "SAWTOOTH" PATTERN IN ITEM PERFORMANCE

Differences in performance on new and reused items and trends in item scores as items are reused can be combined to see whether performance shows the sawtooth pattern noted earlier: a pattern in which item scores increase with reuse, but those gains are not replicated by new items when they are introduced. These patterns were checked for mathematics and reading in grades 4 and 8 from 1993 to 1995. Each comparison was carried out twice: once with all items, and a second time with only matrix items. Because, with but a few exceptions, only matrix items were used to equate KIRIS from year to year, the sawtooth comparisons using only matrix items are most directly relevant to the possible inflation of KIRIS scores. Comparisons involving all reused items, however, may still be informative. Increases in performance on common items excluded from equating may shed light on the nature of student preparation for KIRIS and could contribute to the relative score gains of specific schools even if they could not contribute to statewide increases in KIRIS scores.

The sawtooth pattern appeared to some degree in most cases, although there were exceptions. In some cases, the sawtooth was more striking when all items were considered, but it also appeared when only matrix items were considered.

The sawtooth pattern is illustrated most clearly by the case of eighth grade mathematics, considering all items (Figure 30). The leftmost line in Figure 30 shows that the mean score on items newly introduced in 1993 increased slightly from 1993 to 1994. Performance on items introduced in 1994 was appreciably lower but increased substantially with reuse in 1995. Performance dropped again on items newly introduced in 1995.[2] The

___

[2]In all of these analyses, the 1993-to-1994 and 1994-to-1995 lines are based solely on items introduced in the earlier year and reused in the second year (set 2 for 1994 and set 2 for 1995). For example, the initial point in the 1994-to-1995 trend is the 1994 mean on 1995 set 2 items. We could not do this for the "new in 1995" data points, however, because we did not have the data needed to define 1996 set 2. Therefore, the mean for new items in 1995 reflects set 1 for 1995, which would include any items newly introduced in 1995 that were not reused in 1996. Because 1993 scores were on a different

same pattern appears when only matrix items are considered, but several of the differences are smaller (Figure 31). Here again, the size of these differences (which are drawn from results presented earlier) can be gauged by comparison to the variability of item means. Generally, the means of most new items fall within a range of 0.4 to 0.5 point, so some of the differences in Figure 31 are sizable by comparison.[3]

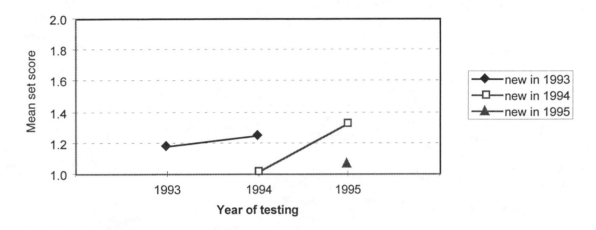

Figure 30—Sawtooth Pattern: KIRIS Grade 8 Mathematics, All Items

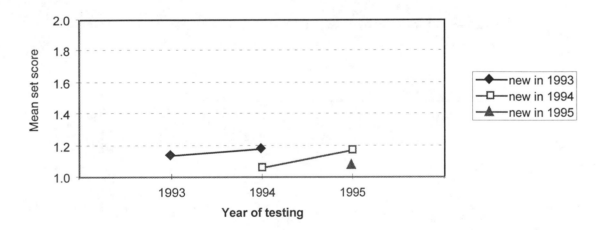

Figure 31—Sawtooth Pattern: KIRIS Grade 8 Mathematics, Matrix Items Only

---

scale, 1993 means were estimated by subtracting from 1994 means on the new scale the difference between 1994 and 1993 means on the old scale.

[3]All figures illustrating the sawtooth pattern have a scale ranging from 1.0 to 2.0 so that any given amount of change has the same appearance in every graph. Since some sets are easier than others, however, this makes the amount of change appear small relative to the scale of the graph.

The other comparisons generally conformed to the sawtooth pattern, but each included one exception. For example, in fourth-grade reading, the two trend lines conformed to expectations, but the new items in 1995 were easier than expected (Figure 32). In fourth-grade mathematics, the two trend lines again conformed to expectations, but when only matrix items were considered, the mean for the new items in 1995 was identical to the mean for reused items that had been introduced the year before (Figure 33). Eighth-grade reading (Figure 34) was similar to fourth-grade mathematics, but there was no increase in mean eighth-grade KIRIS reading scores in 1995, so the lack of contrast between the results on new and reused items in that case is not surprising.

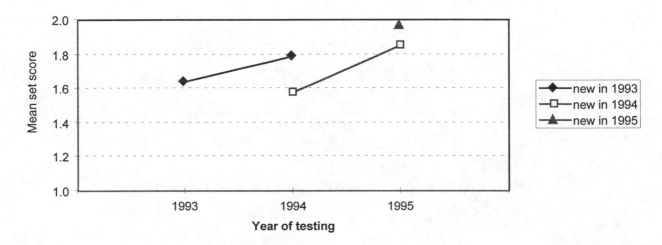

Figure 32—Sawtooth Pattern: KIRIS Grade 4 Reading, Matrix Items Only

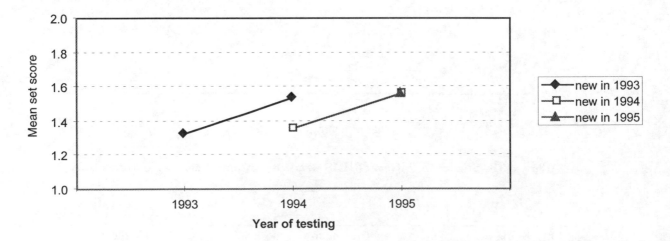

Figure 33—Sawtooth Pattern: KIRIS Grade 4 Mathematics, Matrix Items Only

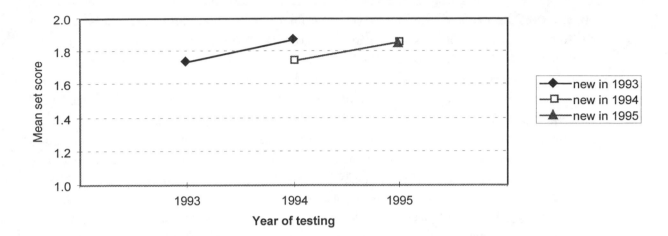

Figure 34—Sawtooth Pattern: KIRIS Grade 8 Reading, Matrix Items Only

In sum, most of the comparisons show a sawtooth pattern that is consistent with coaching, but they are not in themselves conclusive. There were exceptions, and some of the differences were modest in size. Moreover, it remains possible that the evolution of KIRIS led to the development of systematically harder items over time. Nonetheless, the relatively consistent patterns that emerged here are grounds for concern about the validity of gains.

VARIATIONS IN THE DISCREPANCIES IN PERFORMANCE ON NEW AND REUSED ITEMS

Variations in the discrepancies in performance on new and reused items can also provide evidence bearing on the validity of score gains. One of the forms of coaching that could produce gains in scores that fail to generalize to other tests could be called item-specific coaching: having students practice tasks very similar to items that will be reused, or even practicing the items themselves. The effect of this item-specific coaching would be to raise students' performance on reused items relative to new items. The better performance of Kentucky students on reused items could reflect item-specific coaching but is not sufficient evidence of it, because the performance difference could stem from other factors as well, such as true differences in item difficulty or other forms of coaching.

A stronger indicator of coaching tailored specifically to reused items would be an association between gains on KIRIS and the performance discrepancy on new and reused items—called a "discrepancy measure" here. That is, was performance on reused items—relative to new items—particularly strong in schools that showed relatively large gains on KIRIS scores?

While an association between KIRIS gains and discrepancy measures would suggest coaching, the lack of such an association need not imply an absence of coaching. Item-specific coaching might be widespread, for example, and only modestly greater in high-gain schools. In addition, it might be that some high-gain schools use an atypical amount of item-specific coaching, while other schools achieved unusually large gains through strengthened instruction, other forms of coaching, or yet other approaches. For example, teachers may focus unduly on the details of scoring rubrics, a practice which has been dubbed "rubric-driven instruction" (Stecher and Mitchell, 1995). If that focus is sufficiently narrow, it may produce gains on the assessment used for accountability that do not generalize well to other assessments. One ongoing study in Kentucky found rubric-driven instruction; specifically, it found a group of Kentucky science and social studies teachers "trying to figure out which type of [opening] sentence led to the highest score" (Hoffman, 1997). Thus, the lack of a strong relationship between discrepancy scores and overall score gains need not imply that coaching in general or item-specific coaching in particular was an unimportant source of gains. The presence of such a relationship, however, does suggest that coaching tailored to reused items may have inflated score increases.

The possible relationship between discrepancy scores and overall score gains was approached in two ways. First, gain in 1994 and 1995, measured as the school mean gain from the previous year on the subject-specific index, was correlated with each of two discrepancy measures: set 1 (new items) minus set 2 (items used for a second time), and set 1 minus set 3 (items reused at least twice). These correlations were explored for all schools with 20 or more students tested in the relevant grades and subjects. Correlations were examined in reading and mathematics in grades 4 and 8, with the exception of grade 8 reading in 1995, when there was no overall increase in KIRIS scores. Second, the size of discrepancy measures was contrasted for high-gain and low-gain schools. To identify these, schools were ranked in terms of their gain in mean KIRIS scores in each subject in each year. Schools in the top quintile of that ranking were classified as high gain; those in the bottom quintile were classified as low gain.

Overall Correlations Between Score Gains and Discrepancy Measures

In reading, there was no general tendency for large gains on the KIRIS index to correlate with large discrepancies in performance on new and reused items. The correlations were inconsistent in sign and were mostly trivial (Table 26). Only one result, the correlation between the 1995 gain in grade 4 and the discrepancy between set 2 and set 1, was statistically significant at better than the 0.05 level after correcting for multiple comparisons. This correlation was negative, however, meaning that schools with *low* gains tended to have larger discrepancies between performance on set 2 items and performance on set 1 items. This correlation was small, despite its statistical significance; with more than 700 fourth-grade schools included, slight correlations reach statistical significance even after adjusting for multiple comparisons.

Table 26

Correlations Between Gain on Index and Discrepancy Measures, KIRIS Reading

	Gain in 1994	Gain in 1995
Grade 4		
Set 2 - set 1	0.06	−0.12
Significance	(ns)	(0.005)
Set 3 - set 1	−0.01	−0.09
Significance	(ns)	(0.07)
Grade 8		
Set 2 - set 1	0.03	NA
Significance	(ns)	
Set 3 - set 1	−0.09	NA
Significance	(ns)	

NOTE: Statistical significance, given here in parentheses, was adjusted for six comparisons using the Dunn-Sidak adjustment.

In mathematics, in contrast, five of the eight correlations showed larger discrepancies in high-gain schools, and there were no appreciable negative correlations (Table 27). All of the five correlations were statistically significant, four highly significant, even after correction for multiple comparisons. None of the correlations was large, but several were appreciable, particularly given the factors noted above that would tend to limit their size. The correlations with gains in the eighth grade in 1995 were the largest.[4]

Table 27

Correlations Between Gain on Index and Discrepancy Measures, KIRIS Mathematics

	Gain in 1994	Gain in 1995
Grade 4		
Set 2 - set 1	0.05	-0.01
Significance	(ns)	(ns)
Set 3 - set 1	0.15	0.18
Significance	(0.000)	(0.000)
Grade 8		
Set 2 - set 1	0.07	0.26
Significance	(ns)	(0.000)
Set 3 - set 1	0.21	0.30
Significance	(0.001)	(0.000)

NOTE: Statistical significance, shown here in parentheses, was adjusted for eight comparisons using the Dunn-Sidak adjustment.

---

[4]The correlation with the set 2 discrepancy was influenced by a single outlying school with the highest score on both measures and would drop from 0.26 to 0.18 if that one school were dropped. The correlation with the set 3 discrepancy, in contrast, would rise modestly, from 0.30 to 0.32, if the most atypical school were removed.

The correlation between KIRIS gains and the set 3 discrepancy measure in grade 8 in 1995—the strongest of these relationships—is shown graphically in Figure 35. The line is the simple regression predicting the discrepancy measure from schools' mean KIRIS gains. The corresponding but more modest correlation for grade 4 in the same year is shown in Figure 36.

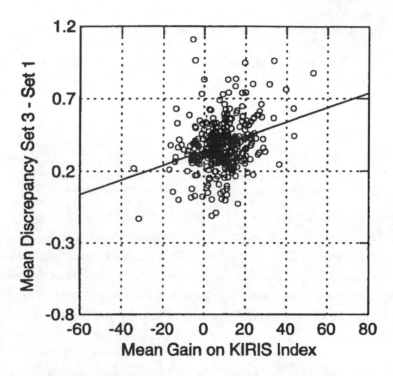

**Figure 35—Correlation Between Mean School Gain and
Discrepancy Measure, KIRIS Grade 8 Mathematics, 1994-95**

Discrepancy Measures in High- and Low-Gain Schools

To further clarify these relationships, discrepancy measures were compared for schools showing relatively large and relatively small gains in KIRIS scores. The following steps were taken to contrast these schools:

1. High-gain schools were defined as those in the top quintile in terms of gain on a subject-specific KIRIS index for a particular year. Low-gain schools were similarly those in the lowest quintile. Thus, in any grade and subject, only a total of 40 percent of all schools entered into the analysis. The 40 percent differed from one analysis to another; for example, a school that was categorized as high gain in reading in 1994 might not be classified as high gain in mathematics in that year or in reading in 1995.

2. School means on each item set were aggregated for high- and low-gain schools, creating means for high- and low-gain schools on set 1 (new items), set 2 (items used twice), and set 3 (items used three or more times).

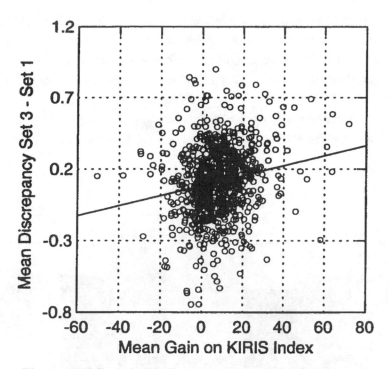

Figure 36—Correlation Between Mean School Gain and Discrepancy Measure, KIRIS Grade 4 Mathematics, 1994-95

3.   For each type of school, the mean differences in performance on new and reused items were calculated. In each case, there were two differences: set 2 minus set 1, and set 3 minus set 1.

4.   These differences were compared across types of schools to see whether the performance difference between new and reused items was larger in high-gain schools than in low-gain schools. A greater difference in high-gain schools— called a "disparity" here—indicates that high-gain schools are performing better on reused items than are low-gain schools, even after taking into account the typically better performance of high-gain schools on new items. In other words, scores on new items are used to hold constant differences in performance between high- and low-gain schools.

5.   In order to judge their size, these disparities were all standardized by dividing them by the standard deviation of school means (for all schools) on the new items.

A finding that high-gain schools outperform low-gain schools by a larger margin on reused items than on new items—that is, the disparity measures are positive and sizable—might suggest that high-gain schools are accomplishing their unusually large score gains in part by coaching tailored to reused items.

To clarify these steps, they are illustrated here with grade 8 mathematics in 1994. Both high- and low-gain schools had very low mean scores on new items: 0.9 for high-gain schools, and about 0.6 for low-gain schools.   Both groups of schools did much better on set 2 items, that is, those that were used for the second time in 1994. This mean performance difference on new and reused items was only slightly larger in high-gain schools than in low-gain schools (Figure 37). However, the mean performance difference between new items and set 3 items, that is, those used for the third time in 1994, was appreciably larger in high-gain than in low-gain schools. The disparity between high- and low-gain schools in the size of the set 3 minus set 1 difference was only 0.15 point, but that seemingly small difference was large compared to the variability of school means on set 1 items: about 0.6 standard deviation.

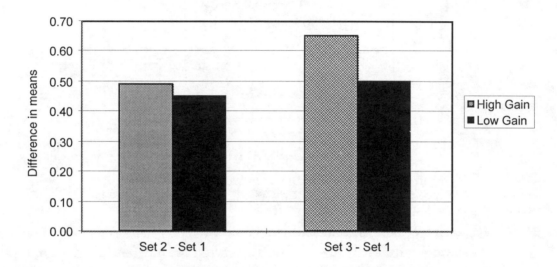

Figure 37—Differences on Item Sets, KIRIS Grade 8 Mathematics, High- and Low-Gain Schools, 1994

As one would expect from the analysis of overall correlations above, the corresponding analysis of reading showed no relationship between disparities and gain. The standardized disparities between high- and low-gain schools were inconsistent in direction and were typically small (see Table 28). Only a single standardized disparity was statistically significant after correction for multiple comparisons. That disparity, while modest, ran in the contrary direction: the gap was smaller in high-gain schools.

The results for mathematics, in contrast, tended to show larger disparities in high-gain schools. In all four of the grade-by-year combinations, at least one of the two disparity measures was equal to or greater than 0.4 standard deviation, and three of the eight instances were 0.5 standard deviation or greater (Table 29). When standardized, the largest disparity, 0.6 standard deviation, was the set 3 minus set 1 difference in grade 8 mathematics shown for illustration above, in Figure 37. All of the sizable differences were larger disparities in high-gain schools, and all of the disparities involving sets 3 and 1 were statistically significant even after correction for multiple comparisons.

Table 28

Disparity in Item Set Means Between High- and Low-Gain Schools, KIRIS Reading

	High-Gain	Low-Gain	Standardized Disparity[a]	Significance[b]
Grade 4				
1994				
set 1	1.7	1.4		
set 2	2.0	1.7	0.1	ns
set 3	2.0	1.7	0.1	ns
1995				
set 1	2.2	1.7		
set 2	2.1	1.7	−0.3	0.03
set 3	2.5	2.1	−0.2	ns[c]
Grade 8				
1994				
set 1	2.0	1.6		
set 2	2.2	1.8	0.1	ns
set 3	2.2	2.0	−0.2	ns

NOTE: Data for 1995 for grade 8 are omitted because there was no overall gain in KIRIS scores in reading in that year.

[a]A positive entry in this column indicates that the performance gap between new and reused items was larger in high-gain than low-gain schools.

[b]Statistical significance adjusted for six comparisons using the Dunn-Sidak adjustment.

[c]p = 0.03 before adjustment for multiple comparisons.

Table 29

Disparity in Item Set Means Between High- and Low-Gain Schools, KIRIS Mathematics

	High-Gain	Low-Gain	Standardized Disparity[a]	Significance[b]
Grade 4				
1994				
set 1	1.8	1.2		
set 2	1.9	1.3	0.1	ns
set 3	2.0	1.3	0.4	0.002
1995				
set 1	1.8	1.5		
set 2	1.9	1.5	-0.1	ns
set 3	2.0	1.5	0.4	0.0004
Grade 8				
1994				
set 1	0.9	0.6		
set 2	1.4	1.1	0.2	ns
set 3	1.6	1.1	0.6	0.008
1995				
set 1	1.2	0.9		
set 2	1.5	1.2	0.5	ns[c]
set 3	1.7	1.3	0.5	0.01

[a]A positive entry in this column indicates that the performance gap between new and reused items was larger in high-gain than low-gain schools.

[b]Statistical significance adjusted for eight comparisons using the Dunn-Sidak adjustment.

[c]p = 0.03 before adjustment for multiple comparisons.

In sum, the two approaches to the discrepancy analysis yielded consistent findings. In mathematics, the discrepancy between new and reused items tended to be larger in high-gain schools, a pattern consistent with the hypothesis of item-specific coaching. In contrast, neither analysis showed such an association in reading.

10. CHARACTERISTICS OF KIRIS AND NONGENERALIZABLE GAINS

If Kentucky's accountability system has generated gains that do not generalize well to other tests—as the limited data presented here suggest—what characteristics of the KIRIS assessment might have contributed to that outcome? There are two reasons to probe this question. First, the implications of a lack of generalizability may depend on its causes. For example, if gains do not generalize because KIRIS includes types of items unlike those included in other assessments, the interpretation of these gains depends on how users define the domains of performance KIRIS is supposed to represent. Second, the causes of nongeneralizable gains may hold lessons for policymakers and educators building other assessment and accountability systems.

This chapter discusses two possible influences on the generalizability of KIRIS gains. The first is a number of aspects of the design and administration of the assessment, such as the methods used to equate scores from year to year. The second is the characteristics of items, particularly those that showed unusually large gains.

THE DESIGN AND ADMINISTRATION OF KIRIS

Numerous aspects of the design and implementation of KIRIS might have had an influence on the generalizability of gains.

The Structure of Test Forms

If assessments are modified substantially over time, there is a risk that apparent changes in performance will actually reflect the effects of these modifications. This risk comes into play not only with changes in the content or format of assessments, but also with changes in administrative procedures, the design of test forms, and so on. The effects of modifications cannot always be predicted and are sometimes larger than anticipated. Analyses of the 1986 NAEP "reading anomaly," for example, suggested that seemingly minor procedural and administrative changes caused large changes in observed performance and substantially biased estimates of trends (Beaton, et al., 1990; Haertel, et al., 1989).

The structure of the KIRIS assessments was repeatedly and substantially modified during the period considered here. The changes were particularly substantial in reading. In fourth grade, the 1992 reading forms began with four passages, each followed by anywhere from three to ten multiple-choice questions. These were then followed by an open-response section with two questions that referred to the first and second passages, even though the questions appeared in the booklet after the fourth passage. These questions were followed by six more passages, again with three to ten multiple-choice questions following each passage. The forms ended with two more open-response questions referring to the fifth and ninth passages.

In 1993, this structure was considerably simplified. Eight passages each had two to six multiple-choice questions and one open-response question appearing immediately after the passage. One passage did not have an open-response question associated with it. This structure was maintained in 1994. In 1995, the multiple-choice questions were dropped, leaving seven open-response questions, each occurring immediately after the relevant passage.

Eighth-grade reading was similar to fourth-grade reading in 1992 and 1993. In 1994, however, the simplification introduced in 1993 was abandoned, and the complex structure of 1992—with open-response questions separated from the prompts to which they referred—was reintroduced for one year. In 1995, multiple-choice questions were deleted, and each open-response question was placed immediately after the relevant passage.

Changes in mathematics were less extensive. In fourth-grade mathematics, forms used in the 1992 assessment had 15 multiple-choice questions followed by four open-response questions and then 40 more multiple-choice questions. In 1993 and 1994, the number of open-response questions was increased, the number of multiple-choice items was decreased, and the open-response items were put in two locations per form. Sixteen multiple-choice questions were followed by three open-response, 12 multiple-choice, and four more open-response items. In 1995, all multiple-choice items were dropped, leaving seven open-response items per form. The changes in eighth-grade mathematics were similar except that the number of items was in some cases slightly different.

An additional change in structure involved the mixing of subject areas. In the first two years of the assessment, all items in a given subject area were placed together. In 1994 and 1995, however, a small number of items were placed among items from other subject areas. This was done in both years with fourth- and eighth-grade reading items and fourth-grade mathematics items. Eighth- and eleventh-grade mathematics items were also switched in 1994. In 1995, for example, one of the fourth-grade reading items was placed in the mathematics section of a form, and one was placed in the social studies section. This was done in an effort to more closely balance the reading levels of the forms.

While modifications of this magnitude could have appreciably affected KIRIS scores, neither the size nor the direction of the effects of these changes, alone or together, is clear. Some might have raised scores relative to underlying proficiency, while others may have lowered scores or had little effect on them. Nonetheless, in some years, trends may have been appreciably biased by them.

Editing of Items

KIRIS items were sometimes edited when they were reused. In principle, items that underwent "major" edits were treated as new items in the next administration. That is, the edited and previous versions were not linked to each other when KIRIS was equated from year to year so that the effects of editing would not bias aggregate changes in KIRIS scores. Items that underwent "minor" edits, however, were treated as the same item and were linked from year to year. If these rules were followed precisely, items that had major edits would not contribute to statewide trends in scores, while those items that had minor edits could contribute. The apparent severity of editing, however, does not necessarily predict its actual impact on scores. Seemingly minor changes might alter performance substantially, while apparently major changes might have little impact. Regardless, the small number of items used in linking increases the risk that edits will bias trends. We therefore examined all items in two subjects that showed particularly large gains—grade 8 mathematics and grade 4 reading from 1994 to 1995—for editing of the items themselves or their scoring rubrics.[1] We examined edited items to see whether they showed greater changes in performance than did other items.

Only a few of the edited items showed particularly large gains in performance, and as a group, edited items showed *less* change than other items did. In grade 8 mathematics, the mean change was about 0.2 point on edited items and about 0.3 on others. In grade 4 reading, even though most of the high-gain items were edited, the mean change was about 0.3 point on all edited items and about 0.4 on others. The magnitude of the increase in item scores seemed in general to be hard to predict from the type of editing we found, but few of the edited items have been released, so we cannot display or describe most of them here to let the reader evaluate the editing.

Thus, in these two subjects, the use of items that had undergone "minor" edits in the linkage of scores, while risky in principle, appears not to have inflated score gains appreciably.

Reuse of Items

The KIRIS design calls for the reuse of most open-response items from one year to the next. A smaller number of items are released to the public and are replaced the following year by new items. Educators are expected to keep secure all items that are not released and can be reused.

In combination with the relatively small number of open-response tasks included in the assessment, this design may make it practical for teachers to remember test content and focus unduly on it, rather than on the domain as a whole. That is, despite test security, it may be feasible to coach students in ways that would not generalize well past the items in the assessment. This potential was particularly great when the test included no multiple-choice items. Even with matrix sampling, which substantially increases the number of tasks in the assessment, the number of items teachers would need to recall was small. For example, in 1994-95, the assessments in core subject areas of mathematics, reading, science, and social studies included a total of 29 tasks in grade 4 and 30 tasks in grades 8 and 11. There were five common items in grade 4 and six in the other grades. These were readily identifiable from their position in the test form. Teachers who wanted to coach students on the assessment needed only to focus on the matrix items, of which there were 24 in each

---

[1]We compared our findings to documentation provided by KDE and Advanced Systems for Measurement in Education. The documentation was somewhat incomplete and inconsistent, however, so we could not always identify with certainty which items were excluded from equating because of edits.

subject in each tested grade (Kentucky Department of Education, 1997, Tables 3-10, 3-11, and 3-12).

The impact of coaching on KIRIS scores, however, depends not only on the feasibility of remembering items. It also depends on the methods used to link scores from one year to the next. A few important points about this linkage follow.

Methods Used to Link KIRIS Across Years

Whenever an assessment that is modified is used to assess trends in performance, it is necessary to link, or "equate," the resulting scores statistically across years so that a given score in one year has approximately the same meaning as the same score in another year.[2] While equating is a common practice, and the methods for equating are well established, the relevance of equating methods for possible inflation of scores may not be apparent, particularly for lay readers. Accordingly, this section provides a brief, nontechnical description of the equating used for KIRIS and how coaching on reused items would affect the equated scores. Readers who want a more adequate technical discussion of the KIRIS equating methods are referred to the various KIRIS technical reports (e.g., Kentucky Department of Education, 1997, Appendix 9).

KIRIS is scaled using an item response theory (IRT) method. IRT methods are now widely employed in large-scale assessments. For example, both NAEP and the Third International Mathematics and Science Study (TIMSS) were scaled using IRT methods. IRT methods assume that student performance in a given area (such as the assessed components of mathematics) reflects a single dimension of ability and that performance on a given item increases monotonically (that is, it always increases) following a specified mathematical function as student proficiency increases along that dimension. For example, mean scores on any mathematics item should increase continually as total mathematics proficiency (as estimated by the KIRIS mathematics score) increases. Student performance and the difficulty of items are placed on the same scale of ability. The difficulty of an item is characterized by the point on the ability scale at which the probability of a correct answer is 0.5. (For a discussion of IRT models, see Hambleton, 1989.) It is the estimation of item difficulty that appears to hold the potential for score inflation in the KIRIS system.

For our purposes, the KIRIS equating method, which is a conventional IRT approach, has two essential components. First, some reused items are removed from the pool of items that are to be linked across years. One class of items that was excluded from linking, as noted earlier, was items that had "major" edits. A second category was items that had been changed from matrix to common. The reason for the latter exclusion is that common items precede matrix items in the assessment forms. Thus, changing an item from matrix to common requires moving it further forward in the test form, perhaps making it easier

---

[2]In the current psychometric literature, the term *equating* is reserved for the most rigorous linkages of test forms. It is not likely that the linking of KIRIS scores across years has met all of the criteria necessary for it to be called equating in this current usage (see, e.g., Linn, 1993). We use the term here only to be consistent with other published discussions of the linking of KIRIS scores over time.

because students confront it when less fatigued. As noted earlier, these rules were generally followed but were not ironclad; some common items were used in equating because of the need for a larger number of items, and the distinction between minor and major edits appears not to have been tested empirically.

An additional basis for excluding items was an unusual change in performance from one year to the next.   Item scores for the two years to be linked were plotted against each other. Any item that appeared to be an outlier in those plots—that is, any item whose scores were dramatically higher or lower than would be expected given the general relationship in performance between the two years—was excluded. It is important to note that change in performance from one year to the next was not grounds for exclusion; to be excluded, an item had to show *much less* or *much more* change than other items did. To our knowledge, there was no formal criterion specified for these exclusions.

Second, statistical adjustments were used to make the distribution (mean and variance) of the difficulty parameters (that is, the IRT estimates of items' difficulty) the same in one year as in the preceding year. In other words, the method assumes that the difficulty of items remains unchanged in the aggregate, thus treating any change in performance after this adjustment as an indicator of real gains in student proficiency. In order to equate two tests, either the students taking the tests or some items in the tests must be held constant to provide the linkage. Since in most instances, successive KIRIS assessments were never administered to a single population of students, the equating necessarily rested on assuming that the true difficulty of reused items—other than those excluded on the basis of the conditions noted above—remained unchanged.

For our purposes, the key question about this approach was whether it provides sufficient protection against inflated scores from factors such as overly narrow coaching, given the reuse of many items and the relatively small number of items that would need to be remembered in order to coach students.   In a model of this sort, increases in item performance caused by factors other than increased mastery of the domain—that is, other factors that make reused items easier—would inflate scores. This would hold true both for coaching and for editing that made items easier. The mechanism by which scores would be inflated is the misestimation of item difficulty. That is, items would in fact become easier because of coaching, some forms of editing, or other factors other than improved mastery of the domains. The equating method could not distinguish among these factors and would, in effect, adjust away any effects of coaching or editing by making the distribution of item difficulties similar to that of the past year rather than making it lower (easier). This would have the effect of making the new version of the test appear harder than it really is and would therefore make students appear more proficient than they really are, relative to the proficiency estimates from the previous year.

The exclusion of most items that had major edits, most common items, and outlier items would offer some degree of protection against inflation of scores. The first two categories of exclusion drop from the equating any items that might become easier—and thus bias trends in scores—because of changes in test construction. The exclusion of outliers would eliminate some items that might bias score trends because of the effects of unmeasured factors, including coaching focused particularly on those items. However, if coaching or other factors that might contribute to nongeneralizable score gains were focused more broadly on many reused items, the characteristics of rubrics, or other specifics of the assessment, then this form of equating would leave KIRIS scores in the aggregate vulnerable to inflation.

CHARACTERISTICS OF ITEMS

Ideally, examining the characteristics of KIRIS items could clarify the factors that might contribute to both generalizable and nongeneralizable gains. A comparison of items included in KIRIS and in other assessments, as was done for ACT and NAEP mathematics above, might suggest relevant similarities and differences in content and format. Examination of KIRIS items that showed the greatest gain could suggest unusual emphases that might not generalize to gains on other assessments. The characteristics of these items might also suggest topics or skills that teachers particularly emphasize in preparing students for the assessment. Examining the characteristics of KIRIS items might also help clarify how feasible it would be for teachers to coach in ways that might inflate scores—that is, how feasible it would be to focus on the skills and knowledge required by reused items without strengthening mastery of the broader domains that the items are supposed to represent. For these reasons, numerous observers have called for detailed examination of the characteristics of KIRIS items.

Accordingly, we examined items from two cases that showed particularly large gains: grade 4 reading and grade 8 mathematics from 1994 to 1995. In each case, we examined all items used in 1995 that had been reused at least once.

In practice, however, an examination of KIRIS items faces numerous obstacles, some of which would also arise with other, similar assessments. The characterization of items is subjective, and different observers might describe them very differently. In the case of KIRIS, test security prohibits displaying some items or even describing them in detail, so readers are unable to determine whether they agree with our characterization of items.

In addition, the characteristics of test items themselves are sometimes not sufficient to indicate what demands those items pose for students or why students' performance on them changes over time. Many KIRIS items are sufficiently open ended that several different aspects of performance could contribute to higher scores. This complication is exacerbated in the case of items that contain several parts, each of which requires an answer. Scoring rubrics provide additional information about the aspects of performance required for higher scores, and accordingly we examined the rubrics for all items in the item sets described here. However, only examination of samples of student work from different years, in combination with items and rubrics, could provide definitive information on the ways in which changes in student performance raised scores on items. While we did examine benchmark papers to see what aspects of performance were singled out in scoring student work, an examination of representative samples of student work from the two years in question was beyond the scope of this effort.

An additional limitation of this analysis is specific to KIRIS: the small number of items. We examined all 1995 KIRIS items in the two groups that were reused at least once;

items that were new in 1995 or that were discarded after 1994 were not useful, because we had no indication of change in performance on them over time. Only 15 mathematics items and 16 reading items were reused in 1995. Moreover, some of these became common items and were therefore excluded from equating. Additional items were edited between 1994 and 1995, and some of these were also excluded from equating. The items excluded from linking for either of these reasons are not directly relevant to potential inflation of scores, although they may still be useful in illustrating the characteristics of items and possible responses by teachers. Finally, some items that were used in linkage over time were edited in more minor ways, and changes in performance on some of them may have been influenced by these edits. The number of items that were reused and were not made common or edited is very small and provides a very limited basis for conclusions about gains on the assessment.

In the two cases considered here—grade 4 reading and grade 8 mathematics from 1994 to 1995—a simple comparison of item scores for the two years suggests that scores increased more on certain items that were made common, but there is no way to know how much of this performance change can be attributed to position effects per se. In fourth-grade reading, the increase in scores from 1994 to 1995 was related to item position in 1995. In general, the further forward in the form an item was placed in 1995, the greater the gain shown on that item from the previous year. This effect, however, was largely the result of the items that were placed in the first two positions; the other three common items showed gains more similar to those of the items that remained matrix (see Figure 38). Similarly, in eighth-grade mathematics, the items that became common and were placed in positions one and two again showed appreciably more gain than other items that were reused (Figure 39). In this case, two of the five items that became common showed relatively modest gain compared to those that remained matrix.[3] Thus, for present purposes, it may be particularly important to note items that were placed in positions 1 and 2; to be cautious, however, we identify all common items.

Given all of these limitations, analysis of KIRIS items cannot conclusively answer questions about the roots of possible score inflation. If these caveats are borne in mind, however, an examination of KIRIS items can be suggestive.

How Variable Are Item Gains?

In order to analyze the correlates of item-level changes in performance, it is first important to explore the patterns shown by these changes. The patterns shown by item-level gains in performance for grade 4 reading and grade 8 mathematics differed markedly.

In eighth-grade mathematics, performance increased from 1994 to 1995 on all reused items (Figure 40). Scores in 1995 were strongly predicted by scores in 1994 ($r = 0.9$). Nonetheless, the amount of gain varied substantially across items, from a low of 0.09 point to a high of 0.67 point.

---

[3]As noted earlier, there were six common items in each subject in grade 8 in 1995. One of the common mathematics items, however, was a new item and is therefore not included in Figure 39.

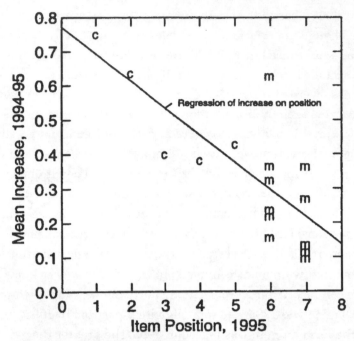

NOTE: The *m* indicates an item that remained matrix; the *c* indicates an item that became common.

Figure 38—Increase in Scores on Reused Items, KIRIS Grade 4 Reading, 1994-95, by 1995 Position and Type

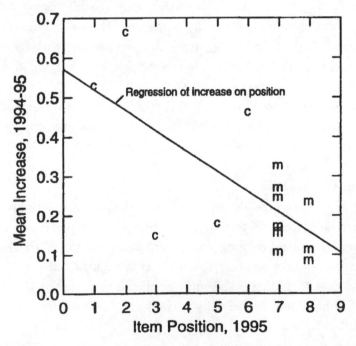

NOTE: The *m* indicates an item that remained matrix; the *c* indicates an item that became common.

Figure 39—Increase in Scores on Reused Items, KIRIS Grade 8 Mathematics, 1994-95, by 1995 Position and Type

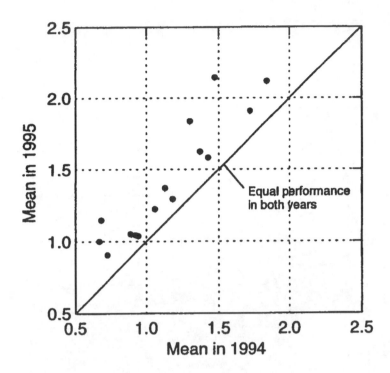

**Figure 40—Mean Scores on Reused Items, KIRIS Grade 8
Mathematics, 1994 and 1995**

In an analysis described earlier, in Chapter 9, the performance difference between sets of new and reused items, called a discrepancy measure, was compared to KIRIS score gains. A correlation between score gains and discrepancy measures might suggest coaching tailored to reused items or other forms of narrowed instruction that could inflate score gains in high-gain schools. Such correlations did not appear in reading but did appear in some cases in mathematics, particularly grade 8 in 1995. In a similar vein, it could be informative to see whether gains on reused items over time were larger in high-gain schools.

As one would expect, all items showed greater increases in high-gain schools. In low-gain schools, the average item-level increase was only 0.05 point, ranging from a loss of 0.1 point to a gain of 0.4 point (Figure 41). The increases in high-gain schools were more variable. They averaged 0.5 point, but they ranged from 0.2 point to almost 1.1 points. Therefore, the disparity in gain between high- and low-gain schools varied from 0.2 point (item 30) to nearly 0.7 point (item 20).

The items with the greatest overall increases tended also to show the largest disparity in change between high- and low-gain schools, but there were many exceptions. This tendency can be seen from Figure 41 but is clearer in a simple scatterplot of the increase shown by each item in all schools versus the difference in change on each item between high- and low-gain schools (Figure 42). The correlation between overall increase and disparity in increase, shown by the solid line in Figure 42, was 0.62. (The numbers of some items are shown in Figure 42 so that readers can identify them in the following discussion.)

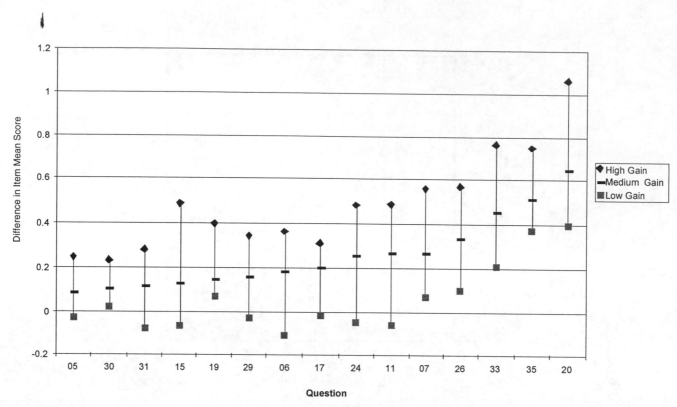

Figure 41—Increase in Performance on Reused Items, KIRIS Grade 8 Mathematics, 1994-95, by Type of School

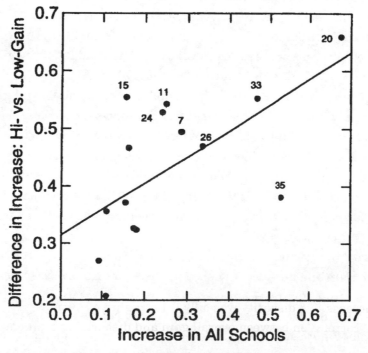

Figure 42—Change on KIRIS Grade 8 Mathematics Items in All Schools vs. Discrepancy in Change Between High- and Low-Gain Schools, 1994-95

Item-level performance changes in grade 4 reading were quite different from those in grade 8 mathematics. In both years, the variability of mean performance across items was smaller in reading than in mathematics (see Figure 43, which has been placed on the same scale as Figure 40 for comparison). The total range of item means in 1994 was 0.7 in reading, as compared to 1.2 in mathematics. The prediction of 1995 item means from 1994 means was somewhat weaker in reading (r = 0.6) than in mathematics, and the item-level change from 1994 to 1995 showed slightly more variability in reading than in mathematics.

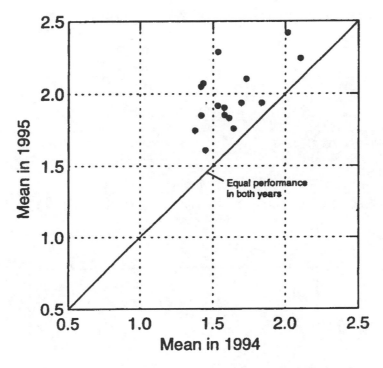

**Figure 43—Mean Scores on Reused Items, KIRIS Grade 4
Reading, 1994 and 1995**

As in mathematics, the reading increases were more variable in high-gain schools. In low-gain schools, the average increase in item means was 0.12 point, ranging from a decline of 0.18 to a gain of 0.48 (Figure 44). The increases in high-gain schools averaged 0.58 point and ranged from 0.27 to 0.98. The disparities between high- and low-gain schools ranged from 0.27 (item 38) to 0.65 (item 27). The average disparity was similar in reading and mathematics, but the disparities varied somewhat less among items in reading.

In reading, unlike mathematics, there was essentially no tendency for high-increase items to show larger disparities in high-gain than in low-gain schools. The correlation between overall increase and disparity was only 0.11 (Figure 45), compared to 0.62 in mathematics. The correlation between overall gain and disparity in mathematics may suggest item-specific coaching—that is, a focus by some teachers on material closely tied to the content of some reused items, leading to both higher overall score gains and larger increases in performance on certain items. If so, however, these results show no appreciable indication of that particular form of coaching in reading, despite the large score increases in reading in that year.

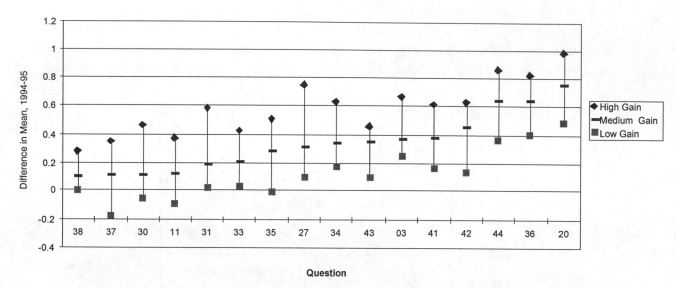

Figure 44—Increase in Performance on Reused Items, KIRIS Grade 4 Reading, 1994-95, by Type of School

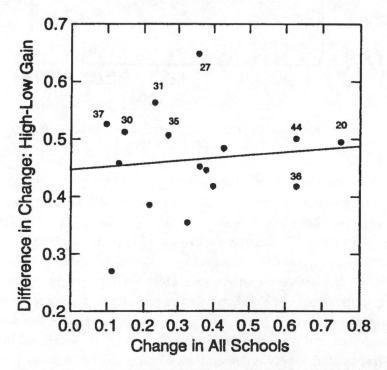

Figure 45—Change on KIRIS Grade 4 Reading Items in All Schools vs. Disparity in Change Between High- and Low-Gain Schools, 1994-95

What Are the Characteristics of High-Gain and High-Discrepancy Items?

Given our concern with the validity of gains, we considered several interrelated characteristics of the items that showed either particularly large overall gains or especially large disparities in improvement for high- versus low-gain schools:

- Whether they are unusual in content or task demands;
- Whether they appear to require highly specific or more generally applicable knowledge and skills; and
- Whether they appear "coachable."

The notion of a "coachable" item warrants clarification. In one sense, all items on an assessment such as KIRIS should be coachable—if performance on an item cannot be improved by changes in teaching, there is no reason to include it in an assessment designed to strengthen instruction. Moreover, KIRIS is intended to provide a signal to teachers about what and how to teach, so it is consistent with the goals of the program for teachers to "coach" students on the knowledge and skills required by the assessment.

Our concern, however, is with types of coaching that would cause increases in performance on specific items (and hence KIRIS scores) without commensurate improvements in mastery of the domains that KIRIS is intended to represent. For example, some teachers might show students "trick" approaches to specific types of problems without teaching them the underlying skills the items are intended to assess. Others may simply focus on the particular content sampled by test items, at the cost of emphasis on other, important aspects of the domains from which those items are drawn. Yet other teachers may focus unduly on patterns in the scoring rubrics—a technique that Stecher and Mitchell (1995) dubbed "rubric-driven instruction." The key issue for our purposes was the extent to which the particular coaching strategies employed led to meaningful and generalizable gains in student performance, as opposed to inflated score gains that do not generalize to other assessments.

While most (if not all) items in assessments of K-12 achievement are likely to be susceptible to undesirable forms of coaching, several characteristics of items and assessments may increase their vulnerability. Easily remembered items would be more vulnerable to this form of coaching, particularly when items are secure (as in KIRIS) and teachers therefore have limited opportunities to see them. For this reason, relatively short items may be more susceptible than many longer items to item-specific coaching. In addition, assessments may be more vulnerable to item-specific coaching when the number of items is small, both because specific items will be easier to remember and because the impact of coaching any one item will be greater. Items are presumably more susceptible to such item-specific coaching when success on them depends on one or a few discrete, easily taught skills or on familiarity with a modest amount of distinct content. Content of that sort would make the item easier to coach, and in many cases, it might also limit the generalizability of performance improvements to other items. Indeed, if the content of an item and the skills it requires are sufficiently unusual, relatively large gains on the item may only be attainable through coaching of a sort that would not produce generalizable improvement in the target domain.

Conversely, certain characteristics may make item-specific coaching less practical or increase the generalizability of its effects to other items. For example, some items may require common content or skills that are likely to appear on other items in the same and other tests, and preparing students for these items may therefore lead to generalizable gains. Other items may be difficult to remember. Long items that require a variety of responses, for example, may be hard to remember in enough detail to coach in undesirable ways. There may be exceptions to this, however, as noted below.

In mathematics, three items showed unusually large gains in performance, ranging from about half a point to two-thirds of a point (items 20, 33, and 35; see Figure 42). None of these three was used in equating, and therefore none could have contributed to score inflation. All three became common items in 1995, and two of the three (20 and 35) were moved to the first two positions on the forms—the placement that appears to make items easier. The remaining item (33) stayed near the end of the form when it was made common, but it underwent a major edit that appears to have made the item easier. However, two of the three (items 20 and 33) were also high-disparity items (i.e., the difference in score increase between high- and low-gain schools was unusually large), which makes it less likely that their increases reflected only factors such as position changes or editing. Thus, it is worth examining them to see what might have contributed to the gains they showed as a way of exploring possible strategies by teachers, even though these items could not contribute to score inflation.

Item 20, which showed the largest increase in performance of any eighth-grade mathematics item and the largest difference in increase between high- and low-gain schools, appears to be a likely candidate for item-specific coaching. It is a spatial visualization task (Figure 17, above). The prompt is memorable, and the three specific requirements of the task are also easily remembered. It requires very specific skills, and those skills would not be expected to increase markedly as a result of either generally strengthened mathematics instruction or general test-wiseness. Indeed, it seems likely that the only way one could generate large gains quickly on this task would be to practice tasks that are very similar. This task is, moreover, unusual, of a sort one would not often find in assessments of achievement. Thus, any gains on this item that did not stem from position changes might have come from teachers focusing narrowly on specific task demands in ways that might contribute to nongeneralizable score gains. The design of KIRIS, however, insured that statewide scores would not be inflated as a result of coaching on this item.

Item 35, which showed the second-largest change in performance, is a much less clear example. It is a mathematical puzzle that is not especially unusual (Figure 46). The item has several attributes that would seem to make it coachable. It is short and easily remembered, and it requires a very specific problem-solving strategy: identifying the one case for which a time is specified, finding another case that can be solved on the basis of the first, then finding one that can be solved on the basis of the second, and so on. On the other hand, this item requires additional skills that should affect performance to some degree on other assessments: basic arithmetic and translating phrases such as "twice as fast" and "25 minutes faster" into arithmetic operations. Thus, even if the gains on this item resulted from teacher behavior and not just the position change, it is not at all clear how much the preparation for this item would produce generalizable and nongeneralizable gains.

34. The children named below ran in the Kentucky Derby Mini-Marathon. The race began at 8:15 a.m. Read the clues below:

  • Ron ran half as fast as Alicia.
  • Bob ran twice as fast as Jerry.
  • Bob finished the race at 9:25 a.m.
  • Ron finished 10 minutes later than Jerry.
  • Elizabeth ran 25 minutes faster than Ron:

List their order of finish and at what time each individual finished the race.

Figure 46—KIRIS Grade 8 Mathematics Item 35, 1994

The remaining items, which showed smaller but still relatively large gains, large disparities, or both (26, 7, 15, 11, and 24; see Figure 42), were all used in equating, so all could in theory contribute to score inflation at the state level. All five are secure items, so they cannot be displayed or described in detail here. They are mostly quite brief and memorable, although one (item 15) might be difficult for teachers not well versed in mathematics to remember. Another (item 24) requires knowledge that is common in elementary and middle-school mathematics curricula, but several of them require more unusual knowledge. For example, item 26, which showed the largest gain of any of these items, is an unusual item that can be solved easily only with highly specific knowledge that few students would have. (Indeed, the wording of the problem implies that the authors expected many students not to have this knowledge.) It appears extremely unlikely that general improvements in mathematical knowledge would produce a large increase on this item or that coaching aimed at improving performance on this item would generalize to gains on other assessments. Item 11 requires students to find the area of a polygon as a multiple of the area of another, smaller polygon and to explain the method of solution. While this is not unusual content on its face, the problem has a "trick" aspect that makes it more difficult than many similar problems, and explaining that specific element would make the problem substantially easier.

One of these five items (15) warrants particular consideration in the context of possible inflation of scores. It is an example of the pattern-recognition-and-extension type noted above that is common in the KIRIS mathematics assessments. The student must extend a pattern; this can be done by drawing on the answer sheet and does not require formal mathematics. The student must then perform two tasks based on the extended pattern, one requiring only simple arithmetic and the other requiring pattern recognition. The pattern shown in the prompt itself is simple and is well known in mathematics. This item could be coached either in task-specific ways or in ways that might contribute to more-generalized improvements in pattern recognition and extension. Given the high frequency with which such items appear to be used in KIRIS, however, even the latter form of preparation might contribute to score gains that do not generalize well to other assessments of mathematics.

Reading is quite different from mathematics in several respects. The nature of KIRIS reading items in grade 4 is illustrated by items 20 and 44 (Figures 47 and 48, respectively), which are the only items showing unusually large increases or disparities in increases that have been released and hence can be displayed or described in detail. First, as both items show, KIRIS reading items generally use relatively long reading passages for students of this age. Second, they require substantial writing. Third, the questions often ask students to refer back to parts of the passage. These requirements are reflected in the scoring rubrics. For example, the 1995 rubric for item 20 assigns a score of 1 to a "vague response that indicates only limited understanding." A score of 2 requires a response that shows "a basic understanding but . . . weak or limited reasons." A score of 3 requires "a complete understanding of how the poets feel . . . but less significant examples . . . and may or may not comment on all three poems." A score of 4 requires an "in-depth understanding that the poets feel a joyous enthusiasm" and "gives significant examples from all three of the poems and/or offers insightful generalizations" (Advanced Systems for Measurement in Education, 1995). Other items impose different specific requirements—for example, they use different types of text, ask different numbers of questions, and ask for different types of detail—but these three attributes are characteristic of the assessment.

As noted, neither of our discrepancy analyses, reported above, found evidence in aggregate scores that would point to successful, item-specific coaching targeted specifically at reused items. Some such coaching might have occurred nonetheless; for example, it might have occurred with similar impact in low-gain as well as high-gain schools. Thus, it is worth considering how amenable items of this sort might be to item-specific coaching.

Items with the characteristics of the KIRIS reading items, such as long reading passages, might appear less amenable to item-specific coaching than some of the mathematics items discussed above. Most of the reading items are much longer than the mathematics items, and it would therefore be more difficult to remember their details. They also rely to a substantial degree on generic skills, such as reading comprehension and writing skills. Nonetheless, coaching appears feasible for some of the KIRIS reading items. Some of the prompts, such as item 44 (Figure 48), present content that is presumably novel to most students at that grade level, and the questions appended to the prompts require that students recall and comprehend that content. Teachers could give students lessons on that content—while still not teaching the specific item—and thus make the material less novel to students. In the case of item 44, that lesson could present the nature of shock and the basic first aid for treating it. Presenting such lessons could substantially increase performance on items such as item 44 without improving reading ability, because students could rely on their memory of the content from a lesson rather than their comprehension of the item's prompt. Even some items that do not require specific content knowledge could be coached by this approach. For example, item 20 (Figure 47) would seem not to require specific content knowledge that is independent of the prompt, and teaching the prompt itself would be a clear violation of appropriate testing practices and KDE's guidelines (although it may have

The three poems you are about to read tell how the poets feel about spring. Read them and then answer question 1.

Spring

I'm shouting
I'm singing
I'm swinging through trees
I'm winging sky-high
With the buzzing black bees.
I'm the sun
I'm the moon
I'm the dew on the rose.
I'm a rabbit
Whose habit
Is twitching his nose.
I'm lively
I'm lovely
I'm kicking my heels.
I'm crying "Come dance"
to the freshwater eels.
I'm racing through meadows
Without any coat
I'm a gamboling lamb
I'm a light leaping goat
I'm a bud
I'm a bloom
I'm a dove on the wing.
I'm running on rooftops
And welcoming spring!

Karla Kuskin

"Spring," from *Dogs and Dragons, Trees and Dreams* © 1958. "Spring" originally appeared in *In the Middle of the Trees* copyright © 1958 by Karla Kuskin. Reprinted by permission of HarperCollins Publishers.

Figure 47—KIRIS Grade 4 Reading Item 20, 1995

Spring Is

Spring is when
the morning sputters like
bacon
   and
      your
         sneakers
           run
              down
                the
                   stairs
so fast you can hardly keep up with them,
and
spring is when
  your scrambled eggs
    jump
      off
        the
          plate
and turn into a million daffodils
trembling in the sunshine.

Bobbi Katz

Good-by My Winter Suit

Good-by my winter suit,
good-by my hat and boot,
good-by my ear-protecting muffs
and storms that hail and hoot.

Farewell to snow and sleet,
farewell to Cream of Wheat,
farewell to ice-removing salt
and slush around my feet.

Right on! to daffodils,
right on! to whippoorwills,
right on! to chirp-producing eggs
and baby birds and quills.

The day is on the wing,
the kite is on the string,
the sun is where the sun should be –
it's spring all right! It's spring!

N. M. Bodecker

Please answer question 1 in the space on page 3 of your Student Response Booklet.

1. How do you think the poets feel about spring? Explain what in the poems makes you think that this is how the poets feel.

Figure 47 (continued)

Read the following article to find out what to do about shock and then answer question 2.

Do You Know What to Do About Shock?

What do the following people have in common?

- Mr. Ruiz broke his ribs in a fall while cleaning the gutters.
- Connie broke her arm playing soccer.
- Jamie cut his hand badly while making a sandwich.
- Mrs. Goldman suffered a head injury in a car accident.

What do the above people have in common? Besides being injured, they could *go into shock* as a result of their injury. When a person is injured, something happens to the circulatory system. In many cases, the system fails to pump enough blood to every part of the body. If shock goes untreated, a person may die. Anytime a person has been injured, it is possible for him or her to go into shock. For that reason, when giving first aid for an injury, you must also treat for shock.

How Do You Know When a Person Is in Shock?

Look for:

Eyes – Blank, dull, pupils dilated (the dark center becomes very large)

Skin – Pale, clammy (moist and cold), blue lips and nail beds

Breathing – Rapid, shallow, irregular

Pulse – Rapid, weak, or absent

Complaints – Thirst, nausea

Emotional State – Slow to answer questions, confused, fearful

Shock is a life-threatening condition. It is important to take care of first things first. Here's what you should do:

- *Call EMS (Emergency Medical Services) immediately.* In most communities, the number is 911.

- *Check airway.* If the person is not breathing, give rescue breathing or quickly locate someone who can. For breathing victims, be sure the airway is open. Clear the mouth of food or other objects. Open the clothes at the neck and waist to help the person breathe more easily.

- *Treat bleeding.* If the person is bleeding badly, it must be stopped before treatment for shock is given. A severe bleeding injury will make shock worse and can cause death. Take the proper safety measures (gloves, for example) to avoid direct contact with blood.

- *Position the person.* Start by having the person lie flat. In most cases of treating shock, raise the victim's feet 8 to 12 inches. Use a rolled-up blanket, jacket, or other object to raise the feet. This helps bring blood to the most important organs of the body. The feet should not be raised if there is a possibility that the

Figure 48—KIRIS Grade 4 Reading Item 44, 1995

person has a head injury. If a person has trouble breathing after raising the feet, lower them. If a person has trouble breathing lying flat, raise the head and chest slightly. If you're unsure, just keep the person lying flat. Turn the person's head to one side. This will keep the person from choking if he or she vomits.

- *Keep the injured person still*. Broken bones can be painful.

- *Maintain body temperature*. Keep the person warm and dry. Cover with a blanket, coat, or other material at hand to keep the victim warm. Also place blankets, coats, or jackets under the person so heat loss can't occur.

- *Handle gently*. Rough handling can be painful and make shock worse by increasing bleeding.

- *Give no food or drink*. This could cause nausea or vomiting. The person may suck on a clean damp cloth if medical help is far away.

- *Keep treating for shock*. Even if the person starts to feel better, keep the victim lying still and warm. Getting up may worsen shock.

- *Reassure the victim*. Let the person know that help is on the way. Talk in a calm voice. Stay calm.

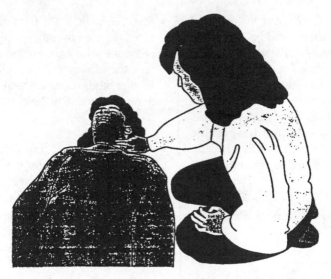

Please answer question 2 in the space on page 3 of your Student Response Booklet.

2. Four accident victims are described at the beginning of this article. Choose any TWO of the victims. Use examples from the article to describe how you would treat each victim you choose.

Figure 48 (continued)

occurred in some cases regardless). But shortly before the date of testing, a teacher could use a lesson in which students read other poems about similar topics—perhaps other poems about happy responses to seasons, or even happy responses specifically to spring—and then answer questions about them similar to those typically asked in KIRIS assessments. In taking the test, students may then recognize the task and recall their responses to the similar examples presented in the lesson.

The three items that showed the largest increases in performance offer little insight into the causes of possible score inflation. Items 20 and 44, which showed the largest gain (see Figure 45), were both moved from the back of their forms to positions 1 and 2, and both were excluded from equating as a result and could not contribute to score inflation. The remaining item with an atypically large overall gain, item 36, remained a matrix item and was included in equating, so changes on this item contributed to changes in overall KIRIS scores. This item cannot be described in detail because it has never been released. It is a long reading passage (longer than item 44) that extends over two and a half pages. It contains illustrations, but even without them would require nearly two pages. The length of the passage would make it very difficult to remember in detail. Students are asked questions about the passage that require them to identify, understand, and explain specific elements in the passage. Unlike item 44, it does not utilize factual knowledge that could be obtained independent of the passage. Item-specific coaching would therefore seem difficult, unless teachers pointed out the needed examples in the prompt itself (a clear violation of Kentucky's policies) or in a very similar prompt. However, the test questions attached to this prompt were edited, and this may help explain the large gain. One question was broken into two separate questions, and the second of these new questions was expanded to point the students to the part of the story in which appropriate examples could be found.

Only one item, 27 (see Figure 45), clearly stands out from the others in terms of the disparity between the score increases in high- and low-gain schools. This item remained matrix and was kept secure, so it cannot be shown here. It was edited, but the change was trivial: "retell the story" became "retell this story." This item does not appear to be a likely candidate for item-specific coaching unless teachers are preparing students in clearly inappropriate ways. It asks students to retell a story that does not include content that would normally be taught. The next four items ranked in terms of disparity, 30, 31, 35, and 37, were all edited, but most of the edits were minor—even trivial—and all but item 31 were used in equating. While some of these items (e.g., 30) depend on content that could be taught separately as a means of coaching, others (e.g., 35) do not. Collectively, they appear to offer few clear clues about the possible origins of nongeneralizable gains.

11. DISCUSSION AND IMPLICATIONS

Because of the complexity of the findings we have described in detail in this report, the first section here provides a brief summary of them and of their limitations. Subsequent sections then discuss their implications for both research and policy.

SUMMARY OF FINDINGS

The validity evidence we presented is of four types: indirect evidence from surveys of teachers and principals, evidence about changes in retention, external evidence from comparisons of KIRIS with other assessments, and internal evidence from analyses of KIRIS itself. It is important to note that this evidence is for the most part limited to the first four years of the program (spanned by the first five administrations of the assessment), from 1992 through 1996. With the exception of the implausibly large gain in eleventh-grade reading in 1997, no evidence bearing on the validity of gains after 1996 is discussed.

Survey Data

Survey data taken alone are not a strong form of validity evidence. Responses to survey questions can be distorted, for example, if respondents have incomplete information or shade their responses toward socially desirable answers. Nonetheless, surveys can provide valuable insights, and survey findings gain credibility when they are consistent with other types of research.

The results of RAND's surveys of fourth- and eighth-grade teachers and principals provide reasons to question the validity of KIRIS score gains. For example, few teachers believed that gains in knowledge and skills—even in the knowledge and skills emphasized by KIRIS—contributed a great deal to the score gains in their own schools, while far more believed that factors such as familiarity with the assessment and use of practice tests had contributed a great deal. Perhaps more telling were the responses of teachers to questions about narrowing of instruction, because these questions asked for statements of fact rather than opinion. The great majority of teachers reported de-emphasizing important parts of the curriculum to focus instruction on KIRIS. To the extent that the de-emphasized material was indeed important for the inferences users draw from KIRIS scores, this practice could lead to appreciable inflation of gains.

Changes in Retention

A long-standing concern about the validity of score gains is that schools can inflate gains by changing the pool of students taking the test. Among the methods often noted in the literature are increasing the assignment of students to special education, changing rules for the exclusion from testing of students with disabilities or limited proficiency in English, being lax about attendance on testing days, and retaining low-performing students in earlier grades so that they are older and more proficient when they reach tested grades.

Most of these potential biases are irrelevant in Kentucky. Because all but the most severely disabled students must be tested and are given scores of zero if they are not, there is no incentive to assign students to special education. Exclusion is permitted only for a small percentage of severely disabled students, who are allowed to produce alternate portfolios in lieu of participating in the main KIRIS assessment, and the rules limiting that option are very strict. Few students in Kentucky are identified as having limited proficiency in English. Allowing low-performing students to be absent accomplishes nothing, because all students enrolled are assigned a score of zero if they are not tested. The only one of these potential biases that appears to have serious potential in Kentucky is retention in grade.

Our analyses of the age distributions of tested students show no evidence of changes that would inflate scores on KIRIS through the spring 1995 assessment. Indeed, the only appreciable change in the age distribution of tested students—in fourth grade—would have tended to depress rather than exaggerate gains. We have not analyzed data relevant to later increases in scores.

External Score Evidence

Ideally, external comparisons to other assessment data would be one of the strongest forms of evidence pertaining to the validity of gains. If other, well-built assessments that are designed to support similar inferences are administered to the same cohorts of students, one would expect a sizable percentage of the gains on the accountability assessment to appear in scores on these other assessments as well. In addition, external comparisons are simpler and more easily understood than some of the internal evidence we examined. In practice, however, the external evidence pertinent to KIRIS has several important limitations. We deemed only two tests useful for this purpose, NAEP and the ACT, and both have limitations.

NAEP provides the best comparison to KIRIS because the KIRIS assessment frameworks were explicitly modeled after NAEP's. In addition, NAEP includes open-response items. On the other hand, NAEP provides a very limited set of comparisons because of the small number of NAEP state assessments. The only available comparisons are fourth-grade reading for the first two years of the KIRIS program and fourth- and eighth-grade mathematics for the first four years of the program.

The comparison between NAEP and KIRIS in reading is unambiguous: while fourth-grade KIRIS scores increased by a remarkable three-fourths of a standard deviation during the first two years of the program, NAEP scores remained unchanged. This clearly calls into question the validity of these early KIRIS gains in reading, but it provides no direct evidence about the more recent gains in grade 4 or about the gains in grades 8 and 11.

Kentucky's NAEP mathematics scores did increase over the first four years of the program, but far less than scores on KIRIS. The KIRIS gains were roughly three and a half times as large as the NAEP gains in the fourth grade and four times as large in the eighth grade. Particularly given that the KIRIS mathematics frameworks were explicitly modeled after NAEP's, these very large disparities in trends strongly suggest considerable inflation of

KIRIS score gains. That is, the KIRIS gains do not generalize well enough to warrant the inference that mastery of the intended domain increased by a similar amount.

The fact that scores increased on both mathematics assessments, however, makes it impossible to say with any precision what share of the gain represents inflation. Some degree of disparity in these trends is inevitable. The degree to which this disparity suggests inflation hinges in part on the inferences users draw from the scores. For some particularly extreme inferences about unusual mathematics skills and knowledge, the meaningful gain might constitute much of the total gain. For other, also extreme inferences tied to the specific content of NAEP, the meaningful (i.e., generalizable) gain on KIRIS might be even less than the NAEP gain—that is, even less than a fourth of the total observed gain.

The intended and likely inferences appear much less extreme, however, and for those inferences, the degree of inflation appears to be sizable. The mathematics assessment was clearly designed to measure much of the same content and skills as NAEP does, and there is nothing to suggest that users expect the test to measure highly idiosyncratic skills and knowledge unlike those measured by other tests of mathematics. Thus, it is reasonable to expect that meaningful gains on KIRIS would have a substantial echo in NAEP trends. To illustrate, even if one argued that one-third of the disparity in trends between NAEP and KIRIS in eighth-grade mathematics should be discounted because of differences in domain specification, item format, and other differences between the assessments, the data would suggest that KIRIS overstated generalizable gains by at least a factor of two.[1]

Comparisons of KIRIS with the ACT are less telling than those with NAEP because KIRIS is less similar to the ACT than to NAEP. The KIRIS high school frameworks were not explicitly designed to reflect those of the ACT, and an examination of the assessment frameworks and of items from the two assessments showed clear differences. For example, KIRIS places much less emphasis than does the ACT on the content of traditional intermediate and advanced high-school mathematics courses, such as intermediate algebra. Moreover, the ACT is entirely multiple choice.

Nonetheless, the frameworks and content of KIRIS and the ACT do show appreciable overlap, and it is unlikely that many stakeholders would argue that gains on KIRIS should have no reflection in ACT scores. Indeed, KDE has itself used cross-sectional correlations between the two assessments as evidence of the validity of KIRIS and has argued that "it is not overly presumptuous to assume that increased learning that leads to improvement on one [of these assessments] is likely to lead to improvement on the other" (Kentucky Department of Education, 1997, p. 14-7). Therefore it seems reasonable to compare trends on KIRIS and the ACT, although the greater difference between the two tests might lead one to accept a larger discrepancy in trends than one would accept with NAEP. Inferences from

---

[1] Observed gains were 0.52 standard deviation on KIRIS and 0.13 standard deviation on NAEP, giving a disparity of 0.39 standard deviation. If one assumes that all of the NAEP increase represents generalizable gains and that one-third of the disparity represents meaningful gains on KIRIS that did not generalize to NAEP because of differences in frameworks, format, etc., then meaningful gain would be 0.26 standard deviation, half of the 0.52 observed.

ACT scores about the validity of KIRIS gains are of course limited to the high-school KIRIS trends.

An additional limitation of the ACT comparison is that it pertains directly only to the students who took the ACT. In our examination, however, ACT trends were compared only to the trends on KIRIS of students who took both tests. This approach protects the internal validity of the comparisons from bias stemming from changes in the selectivity of the group taking the ACT. Because ACT-takers comprised about half of all students tested with KIRIS and exhibited trends on KIRIS roughly similar to those of the state as a whole, the external validity of the comparisons—that is, their generalizability to the state as a whole—also seems reasonable.

In mathematics, the disparity in trends between ACT and KIRIS from 1992 through 1995 (among students who took both tests) was striking: a gain of about 0.7 standard deviation on KIRIS compared to a trivial decline on the ACT. Reading showed a much smaller increase on KIRIS because of a drop in mean scores in 1993, but it still showed a clear contrast: a gain of over 0.33 standard deviation on KIRIS but essentially no change on the ACT.

In both subjects, the lack of any increase on the ACT simplifies interpretation of the disparity. The main questions of interpretation are the degree of overlap between the tests and the nature of the inferences users reach. Because the ACT differs more from KIRIS than NAEP does, it would be reasonable to expect more of the disparity in trends between KIRIS and the ACT than the disparity between KIRIS and NAEP to be a reflection of those differences rather than an indication of an inflation of KIRIS scores. Even if one discounted fully half of the disparities in trends, however, these findings would suggest that KIRIS overstated meaningful gains in mathematics and reading by a factor of two.

ACT science scores are analogous to the NAEP mathematics scores discussed above in that mean scores increased on both tests, but the increase in KIRIS scores was more than four times as large as that on the ACT. The increase on the ACT over the three-year period was a bit less than 0.1 standard deviation, which is a plausible increase for that short a period. The increase in science scores on KIRIS was more than 0.4 standard deviation. If one assumes that fully half of the disparity in trends should be discounted because of differences in frameworks, format, etc., then these data would suggest that the observed science gains overstate meaningful gains by a factor of about 1.7.[2]

Internal Score Evidence

We presented five types of internal evidence:

- A simple comparison of the size of gains with expectations of gains based on other data;

---

[2] The observed gains were 0.43 on KIRIS and 0.09 on the ACT. If one assumes that all of the NAEP increase represents generalizable gains and that half of the disparity represents meaningful gains on KIRIS that did not generalize to NAEP because of differences in frameworks, format, etc., then meaningful gain would be 0.26 standard deviation. The observed gain is 1.66 times this amount.

- Contrasts in performance on new versus reused items within years;
- Changes in performance on reused items over time;
- A "sawtooth" pattern based on the previous two types of comparisons: increases in performance on reused items over time, followed by a decrease in performance on new items; and
- A discrepancy analysis, in which differences in performance on new and reused items (within years) in a given subject were correlated with overall school gains on KIRIS in that subject.

We also presented a sixth, more limited analysis that was similar to the discrepancy analysis but examined changes in performance on reused items over time rather than differences in performance on new and reused items. That is, it examined whether reused items that showed the greatest overall performance increase over time showed larger performance changes in schools that had particularly large gains on KIRIS. This last analysis was carried out in conjunction with the qualitative analysis of the characteristics of items that showed large performance increases.

Our analyses of internal evidence were constrained by numerous factors. For example, the equating methods used with KIRIS provided no clear estimate of the relative difficulty of new and reused items. Item edits and changes of position within forms may have distorted changes in item-level performance over time. While these design decisions can be justified for other reasons, they cloud internal analyses of validity. In addition, methods for analyzing internal data to evaluate the validity of score gains are poorly developed.

Despite these limitations, the analyses of internal data in mathematics were generally consistent with inflation of score gains, albeit with some exceptions. The findings pertaining to reading were less consistent.

In both cases, the simplest internal evidence—the size and rapidity of the observed gains in scores—may be among the most telling. Many of the gains were very large relative to past evidence about large-scale changes in performance, and several were huge. Two gains particularly stand out: the gain of 1.3 standard deviations in fourth-grade reading over the first three years of the assessment, and the gain of 0.66 standard deviation in eleventh-grade reading in a single year (1997). Other notably large gains were the increases of roughly 0.7 standard deviation in fourth-grade mathematics over two years; roughly 0.6 standard deviation in fourth-grade science over two years; roughly 0.6 standard deviation over two years in eighth-grade mathematics; and roughly 0.5 standard deviation over two years in twelfth-grade mathematics.

Meaningful gains of these magnitudes would be highly unusual, but *observed* gains of this size are less surprising. It is common to find large gains in mean scores during the first years of administration of a new assessment, in part because of familiarization. Limited research has shown that these initial gains do not necessarily generalize to other tests (e.g., Koretz, Linn, Dunbar, and Shepard, 1991). One reason for rapid initial gains is simple familiarization with the specific demands of the test. Initial, nongeneralizable KIRIS gains stemming from familiarization would be consistent with the responses of many Kentucky teachers to the RAND surveys.

In mathematics, our results from comparing performance on new and reused items, looking at trends in performance on reused items over time, and analyzing the sawtooth pattern were generally consistent with inflation of gains. There were exceptions, however, and some of the differences were small. New items were harder than reused ones by a small margin in grade 4 but by more substantial amounts in grade 8. All reused mathematics item sets examined showed score increases over time. When these two changes were combined, the resulting sawtooth pattern was clear in grade 8 and had one exception (out of ten means examined) in grade 4.

Because of the uncertainty about the true relative difficulty of new and reused items, we considered the discrepancy analysis to be a stronger form of evidence than analyses based on means across all schools. A greater difference in the apparent difficulty of new versus reused items in schools that show particularly large gains on KIRIS would suggest item-specific coaching, which could be a cause of inflated gains. In mathematics, schools with large gains on KIRIS did tend to show greater differences in performance on new and reused items, although this correlation was modest. Similar differences were clear when high-gain and low-gain schools were compared.

The results for reading were markedly less consistent. In both grades, new reading items were more difficult than reused ones only in one year (1994) of those considered. In most sets of reused reading items, however, performance did increase over time, leading to a sawtooth pattern that had a number of exceptions. Perhaps more important, the association between score gains and the performance difference on new and reused items that appeared in mathematics was absent in reading.

INTERPRETATIONS OF FINDINGS

Taken together, the external evidence and internal evidence suggest clear inflation of score gains in mathematics. Many KIRIS gains were implausibly large, and all external comparisons showed either no increases in mathematics on other assessments or increases that were far smaller than those on KIRIS. Changes in item difficulty over time and differences in performance between new and reused items were generally consistent with a hypothesis of inflation and created a sawtooth pattern—an increase in performance on reused items followed by a decrease in performance on new items—in both grades. Moreover, the modest tendency for the discrepancy between performance on new and reused items to be larger in high-gain schools suggests that item-specific coaching may have contributed to inflation of scores.

The evidence is less clear-cut in reading. The huge observed-score gains in the fourth and eleventh grades are grounds for suspicion, and the external comparisons again suggest inflation, but there were fewer external comparisons to consider in reading than in mathematics. Some of the internal evidence was consistent with inflation of scores, but the exceptions are numerous. In particular, the discrepancy analysis provided no clear evidence of item-specific coaching.

If reading gains were inflated, as the external evidence suggests, but without substantially more item-specific coaching in high-gain schools, then how was the inflation brought about? Our analyses do not provide an answer to this question. Teachers may have engaged in other forms of coaching, such as teaching students strategies designed to capitalize on the scoring rubrics. Anecdotal reports of such approaches are common in Kentucky. We are not aware, however, of any systematic evidence about either the frequency with which such approaches are used or their impact on scores. One other possibility is that item-specific coaching might have occurred, but more uniformly across high- and low-gain schools.

In interpreting the evidence bearing on inflation of gains, one must bear in mind the time period examined. The score gains evaluated here included only the first four years after the first administration of the KIRIS assessment. As noted, scores on new assessments often increase rapidly during the first years of their use, and a substantial portion of those initial gains may fail to generalize to other assessments. Some portion of large initial gains is likely to reflect familiarization with the assessment—that is, students and teachers learning about a new assessment's content, format, and scoring. To the extent that these details are specific to the assessment, the gains that stem from familiarity with them are unlikely to generalize well.

Gains from familiarization may be particularly large when an assessment is innovative and imposes novel demands on teachers, students, or both. The administrative complexities of innovative performance assessments may also exacerbate gains from familiarization. That is, scores may be initially depressed by teachers' uncertainties about the administration of the assessment and may rise as the operation of the assessment becomes more routinized.

Given that large and partially ungeneralizable gains are so common in the first years of an assessment program, is it reasonable to evaluate the extent to which those gains are inflated? Some observers argue that initial, nongeneralizable gains from familiarization are so likely that the better test of an assessment program is the generalizability of gains that occur after the first two or three years. By this logic, nongeneralizable gains on KIRIS through 1994 or even 1995 are to be expected, and the gains thereafter would be a more important target for evaluation.

Whether the initial gains are an important focus for evaluation, however, depends on what users infer from them. If the sponsors and users of an assessment discount the initial gains on the basis that they might be inflated by familiarization, there would be little reason to evaluate their validity. If, however, the sponsors and users present the initial gains as evidence of improved student learning, then it is important to determine whether the public should accept that claim as valid.

In the case of KIRIS, KDE unambiguously presented initial score gains as evidence of real improvements in student learning. KDE presented the gains to the public with titles such as "Celebrate the Progress!" (Kentucky Department of Education, 1995a), and it paid over $20 million in reward money to schools on the basis of those gains. It is thus necessary to evaluate the degree to which the inference was warranted.

It is not clear on the basis of the evidence presented here, however, how much of the problem of exaggerated gains in Kentucky persisted beyond an initial period of familiarization. The lack of statewide score increases in 1996 led some observers to suggest that the period of familiarization had ended by 1995. Gains resumed in 1997, however, and as noted earlier, one of the 1997 gains (that in eleventh-grade reading) not only was one of the largest in the history of KIRIS, but was too large to be plausible. That single instance, however, could reflect any number of factors. The most reasonable conclusion at this point about longer-term gains is that more data will be needed to evaluate them.

IMPLICATIONS FOR POLICY

The pressure for accountability in education is unlikely to abate any time soon, and assessments will continue to be a cornerstone of accountability systems. Accountability is of questionable value, however, if it generates illusory progress in the form of inflated score gains. How might educators and policymakers avoid such marked inflation in the future?

The problem of score inflation is not likely to be solved fully by changes in test format alone. Nearly a decade ago, many policymakers decided that they could avoid the problem of score inflation by relying on test formats other than multiple choice. Inflation of gains, however, need not be tied to a particular format (Koretz, 1996). A performance assessment that is "worth teaching to" in the sense of modeling appropriate instruction can still be vulnerable to score inflation because it still only samples from a broader domain, and teachers can narrow instruction to focus on the sample rather than on the domain as a whole. Indeed, the use of open-response formats may in one way exacerbate the potential for inflated scores by reducing the number of items that can be administered in a given amount of testing time. While evidence from other assessment systems is limited, the KIRIS experience documented here underscores the inability of format, by itself, to protect against score inflation.

Although it may not be possible to eliminate the problem of inflated scores entirely in an accountability system, it may be feasible to lessen its severity and impact. There is no solid research evidence documenting large-scale test-based accountability systems that have circumvented the problem of inflated scores, however, so the following suggestions must be seen as speculative.

Set realistic goals for the improvement of performance. The amount and speed of performance improvements are constrained by factors beyond the control of education policymakers and, in some cases, beyond the immediate control of schools. Noneducational factors such as social background have strong influences on performance, not just in the United States, but worldwide (Beaton, et al., 1996). Many schools lack the capacity to make rapid, large changes in instruction. For example, many teachers lack training in the fields they teach, and some have weak pedagogical training; many schools lack adequate physical facilities; and many schools lack high-quality texts and other materials. These factors are not a justification of the status quo, but they limit the speed at which real learning—that is, student mastery of the domains assessments are intended to represent—can be improved.

Requiring faster changes than teachers can effect by appropriate means may exacerbate the problem of inflated scores. Teachers can improve students' mastery of tested material more rapidly than they can improve mastery of the much larger domains an assessment is intended to represent. If they cannot feasibly increase mastery of the domain rapidly enough, they will have a powerful additional incentive to narrow instruction by inappropriate teaching to the test.

The rate at which performance can be improved will vary from school to school, and policymakers will need to rely on judgment in deciding on targets. Because of the problem of inflated scores, however, they should base those targets on actual information about the distribution of student performance and about the capacities of schools to change. Setting targets without reference to the distribution of performance, as was done in Kentucky, may exacerbate the risk of inflated scores.

Tie assessments to clear curricula. In order to teach to the intended domains rather than to the specific test, teachers need to know what the intended domains are. While this generalization may appear trite, it is often ignored in assessment-based reforms. That is, some reforms lead with an assessment, leaving curriculum to follow later. In some cases, centralized accountability assessments are instituted with an explicit understanding that they will *not* be accompanied by a centralized curriculum.

Instituting a centralized accountability assessment without a clear centralized curriculum also appears to be an invitation to inflate test scores. Both the advantages and disadvantages of centralized curricula are numerous and are for the most part beyond the scope of this report. Instituting a centralized, high-stakes assessment program, however, changes the benefits and costs of a centralized curriculum. Holding teachers accountable for scores on a centralized assessment without specifying the curriculum from which it samples invites them to focus on the assessment as an end in itself rather than on the domains it is intended to represent. Indeed, even if teachers want to resist the temptation and focus on the domains, they would not know what the domains comprise. Guidance comes from the assessment itself, which in effect becomes a surrogate curriculum framework.

In addition to providing clarity about the domains the assessments are supposed to represent, a specified curriculum can also provide a basis for building an assessment program less vulnerable to inflation of gains. Once a curriculum is specified, rules can be created for sampling from that domain for purposes of testing. Teachers can then be told that regardless of what happened to be sampled in building the assessment for one year, anything in the curriculum can be sampled for the assessment in the next year, following the specified rules. The incentive to focus instruction on the previous assessments would thus be reduced. Explanation of the sampling that will be done from year to year to build the assessments could be enhanced by releasing several different prototype assessments rather than a single one, in order to illustrate concretely that assessments would be differing samples from the same domain (Linn, 1997).

Design assessments to minimize inflation. Developers must trade off many competing factors in designing an assessment. These include both measurement concerns, such as content coverage, bias, and various aspects of validity and reliability, and practical concerns, such as student time demands, administrative complexity, and costs for development, materials, and scoring. The trade-offs among these factors differ depending on the assessment's uses. A design that is appropriate for an assessment that has only low-stakes uses may lead to severe inflation of gains if the same assessment is used for accountability.

The Kentucky experience suggests several design strategies that might help reduce the inflation of gains. First, conventional test security rules may be insufficient protection for reused items. Teachers' and students' recollections of previous assessments may make it necessary to limit the proportion of the assessment that is carried over from year to year. This strategy may be particularly important in the case of essay and performance assessments because they entail fewer tasks for a given amount of testing time than a traditional multiple-choice test. Second, when sampling of the domain (for example, sampling of mathematical skills) is necessarily incomplete, it may be important to vary sampling systematically from year to year. That is, if a given year's assessment happens to provide relatively sparse coverage (or no coverage at all) of a given element of the curriculum framework, it may be important to insure that that particular element is covered in a subsequent year's assessment. Third, it may be important not to reuse items that are highly tied to initially novel content that is easily taught. Then, for example, a fourth-grade reading comprehension item that focuses on treatments for shock cannot be undermined by a teacher giving a science lesson on that topic.

The approach to linking assessments from year to year may also need to be chosen with accountability pressures in mind. Two aspects of linking are important: the consistency of the assessment over time and the methods chosen for linking scores.

Observers have repeatedly raised concerns about the meaningfulness of KIRIS score trends because of major inconsistencies in the design of the assessment from year to year (e.g., Hambleton, et al., 1995; Catterall, et al., 1998). Designers of assessments that are intended to measure trends are faced with a tension between maintaining consistency over time and adapting the assessment for various reasons. On the one hand, modifications made to the assessment can threaten the validity of trend estimates, and past experience has shown that the amount of modification needed to distort trends is difficult to predict. On the other hand, it is often impractical to maintain perfect consistency in the assessment over time. As noted, when tests are used for accountability, it may be necessary to limit the reuse of content in order to minimize the potential for inflation of scores. Moreover, it is appropriate for the designers to refine the assessment over time in response to information about its quality and impact, even though changes in design may require evaluation and that new trend lines be started.

Although this tension between consistency and change in assessments cannot be fully resolved, steps can be taken to lessen it. First, designers should avoid unnecessary changes. For example, it was not necessary to change the placement of KIRIS reading questions so that they immediately followed the relevant prompt in some years but not in others. Second, the design of assessments used for accountability should reflect current knowledge about the limitations of testing. Innovative but unproven methods should be considered experimental until data about their quality are in hand.

The methods used to link scores over time may also need to reflect the accountability uses of assessments. The methods used to link KIRIS scores from year to year are not exceptional. They are based on well-known IRT methods, and the specific implementation of those methods was reviewed in recent years by prominent experts in the field. They appear nonetheless to have been insufficient for use in this high-stakes system. The reason appears clear only in hindsight: the accountability pressures made a central assumption of the method—the assumption that reused items remain comparably difficult over time—untenable. No methods for linking scores are likely to be entirely adequate under circumstances such as Kentucky's, but it appears to be necessary to explore a wider range of methods, including some that make no assumptions about stability of item difficulty over time.

Limit interpretation of initial gains. As noted above, the interpretation of initial gains is clouded by the likelihood of inflation from familiarization. One way to address this problem would be to limit interpretations of initial gains, particularly when high stakes raise the risk of inflation. Sponsors could warn the public and other stakeholders that initial gains are likely to be exaggerated by familiarization and that only longer-term gains are likely to be grounds for confident inferences about meaningful improvement in student learning. To our knowledge, no state assessment systems currently present results in this fashion.

Monitor for inflation of gains. The risk of inflated scores, particularly in the first years of assessment programs, is great enough that routine monitoring for inflation of gains in high-stakes testing programs seems appropriate. The methods for carrying out this monitoring need further development, but some steps can be taken at present. Sample-based audit testing, such as is provided by the NAEP state assessment, is one approach, albeit a costly one. Assessments can be designed to provide better internal data than are offered by KIRIS. For example, if items are reused, better estimates of inflation can be obtained from the contrast between new and reused items if they are equated with methods that would not be undermined by score inflation, such as out-of-state common-persons equating (when that is practical). If assessment programs are designed from the outset with these considerations in mind, some of the methods used here—such as the discrepancy analysis contrasting high- and low-gain schools—might be practical on an occasional if not annual basis.

Credit aspects of performance other than test scores. It is not yet clear how much protection against score inflation is offered by changes in the design of assessment programs such as those suggested. Some exaggeration of gains and some unintended negative incentives are likely to remain no matter how well a system is designed, simply because many valued outcomes of education are poorly tested or not tested at all by current assessments.

The larger question posed by inflated scores is therefore the role that test scores and other variables should play in an accountability system. KERA recognized the importance of considering other factors in its use of noncognitive measures, but the measures it considers are limited. There are few of them, and they show relatively little variability and limited room for improvement. Moreover, some of these noncognitive factors (particularly the successful transition to postsecondary education or work) may be substantially outside the control of schools.

Moreover, from the point of view of teachers in many grades making daily or monthly decisions about practice, both the cognitive and noncognitive KIRIS variables may be distant considerations at best. Teachers will often (and appropriately) focus on shorter-term outcomes, such as finding ways to get an unmotivated student interested in a subject or finding clearer ways of presenting particular concepts or factual knowledge, regardless of whether they are likely to be tested. These outcomes may not be reflected measurably in assessments administered several grades later or in coarse noncognitive variables such as transition rates.

Thus, in response to the problem of inflated scores (and the undesirable narrowing and corruption of instruction that it implies), it may be desirable to find ways to broaden accountability systems to focus not just on long-term outcomes, but also on shorter-term outcomes and the quality of practice itself. Methods of incorporating these factors into large-scale, centralized accountability systems are controversial and poorly developed, and designing and testing systems that include them will be a difficult task. Undertaking that task, however, may in some instances be the key to reducing inflation of gains to an acceptable level—and therefore may be the key to producing the gains in student learning that are the goal of accountability systems.

IMPLICATIONS FOR RESEARCH

Although the evidence presented here, taken together, is sufficient to suggest strongly that KIRIS score gains were inflated, it provides a seriously incomplete view of both the extent of the inflation and (particularly in reading) the mechanisms that might have produced it. Clearly, as score gains increasingly become the focus of accountability systems, it will be important to develop stronger methods for evaluating the validity of score gains.

Specification of intended domains. An essential step toward firmer evidence about the validity of gains would be a clear definition of what might be called the "domain of generalization" of assessments. If the generalizability of score gains on accountability assessments to other, less coached assessments is to serve as a primary test of the validity of gains, one should ideally be able to state with more clarity than was done here what patterns of generalization are to be expected. To do so would require a much clearer delineation of assessment domains than has been available to date for KIRIS or for many other large-scale assessments. This specification could be used to interpret the generalization to other tests (such as NAEP) as well as to design evaluations of generalizability specifically for a given assessment.

Design of operational assessments. Clearer evaluation of the validity of gains would also be helped by taking the needs of evaluation into account in designing assessments themselves. Some of the steps that were noted above as ways of ameliorating score inflation would also facilitate the evaluation of gains. For example, deliberate changes in the sampling of content from clearly specified domains would lessen the incentives to teach to the test. By providing a contrast in performance on familiar and novel items, such sampling could also provide valuable information about narrowing of instruction and the validity of gains. The methods of linking assessments across years could also be important. For example, as noted above, there are methods of linking (such as common-population equating of new and reused items) that would lessen inflation of gains from reusing items; those same methods would also provide a much stronger basis for gauging validity from the contrast in performance on new and reused items. A more extreme approach would be to avoid entirely the reuse of items in operational test forms.

Methodological development. The methods used here to assess the validity of gains are limited and crude compared to the methods available for evaluating the validity of performance cross-sectionally. The field of measurement has seen many decades of intensive development of methods for evaluating scores cross-sectionally, but much less attention has been devoted to the problem of evaluating gains. Given the increasing pervasiveness of high-stakes testing and the increasing focus on score gains over time as the basis for accountability, this methodological gap is likely to become ever more important.

Research on the mechanisms underlying score inflation. The contrast between mathematics, in which there was evidence of item-specific coaching, and reading, in which apparent inflation was not accompanied by evidence of item-specific coaching, underlines the limits of our current knowledge of the mechanisms that underlie score inflation.

Some mechanisms of test preparation, such as teachers' narrowing of instruction to de-emphasize untested material, have been documented numerous times (e.g., Koretz, Barron, Mitchell, and Stecher, 1996; Koretz, Mitchell, Barron, and Keith, 1996). Others, such as rubric-driven instruction (e.g., Stecher and Mitchell, 1995), have been recognized only more recently and have been less frequently documented. Overall, there is not a great enough understanding of the range of practices employed and their relationships to both meaningful score gains and inflated scores.

This weakness of understanding with regard to test preparation will be ever more important if education continues to be increasingly dominated not only by high-stakes assessments, but also by assessments that are explicitly intended to model and influence instruction. Some degree of teaching to the test is desirable if tests are used for accountability, and the current focus on "tests worth teaching to" may make desirable forms of teaching to the test more important. To disentangle meaningful from meaningless score increases, however, will require a more refined ability to monitor the types of test preparation used and their effects on both scores and mastery of the intended domains of generalization.

THE KIRIS EXPERIENCE IN CONTEXT

Over the past year, the KIRIS assessment and accountability program has been the focus of intense controversy, and legislation enacted during the past year will lead to substantial (although not yet fully specified) changes. Some readers will look to the evidence presented here for its relevance to that debate. It would be unfortunate, however, to consider these findings only in the context of the debate within Kentucky. Although KIRIS is in some respects unique, it shares key attributes with many assessment and accountability programs around the country. Features such as the focus on aggregate gains, the linking of gains to rewards, the reliance on assessments administered in only a few grades, the attempt to circumvent the problem of teaching to the test by relying on certain formats, the weak specification of curriculum, the reliance on reused test items, and the setting of goals for improvement without reference to actual performance distributions—all of these can be found in varying combinations in other state and local programs. The lack of empirical support for the validity of the rapid score gains observed in Kentucky should serve as a warning to other jurisdictions as well of the risks of inflated scores and the need to evaluate the validity of gains.

Appendix

METHODOLOGICAL ISSUES IN THE ANALYSIS OF KIRIS TRENDS

Analysis of KIRIS trends and comparisons of those to trends on the ACT and NAEP are complicated by a number of methodological issues. Several of the most important are noted here, and the approaches to them used in this report are described.

CREATING KIRIS TREND DATA THAT INCLUDED 1992

Comparing KIRIS trends to ACT and NAEP trends requires building a data series in grades 4 and 8 from 1992 through 1994 and 1996 (the years of the NAEP assessments) and in grade 11/12 from 1992 through 1995.

The most tractable KIRIS data for analysis are the "theta" scores, which form a continuous, approximately normal scale of students' proficiency. Theta estimates are not available for 1992, however, and thus could not be used in comparisons with ACT and NAEP scores. In addition, theta estimates are never used for reporting in Kentucky, and the relationship between theta scores and the scores that are reported is obscure.

As an alternative to theta scores, we chose the ordinal NAPD (Novice, Apprentice, Proficient, Distinguished) scale used in the KIRIS accountability system to report all KIRIS results. We also used the same arbitrary numerical values that KIRIS assigns to the four levels: 0, 40, 100, and 140.

The use of NAPD scores has two drawbacks beyond those common to any ordinal scale. One is that KDE changed the way it created NAPD scores for students starting in 1994. It rescaled the scores from 1993 but not those from 1992. Thus, comparisons with the ACT and NAEP entail two partially overlapping series of NAPD scores: those on the old scale, available from 1992 through 1994, and those on the new scale, available from 1993 on.

The second complication arises from the nature of the increase in KIRIS scores after 1992. Much of that increase consisted of a rapid drop in the concentration of students in the Novice and Apprentice categories. As the concentration of scores dropped, the variance of scores increased markedly. For example, the standard deviation of fourth-grade mathematics scores on the NAPD scale increased by 36 percent between 1992 and 1995.

To address the change in the NAPD scale, we compared the change in mean scores on the two scales for the one two-year period (1993 to 1994) for which both are available for all groups used in comparisons with ACT and NAEP trends. The changes were generally similar. In the mathematics data that we compared to NAEP, the changes on the two KIRIS scales were nearly identical in grade 8, but the change on the new scale in grade 4 was considerably larger (Table A.1). In grade 12, the changes in all three subjects that we compared to the ACT—mathematics, reading, and science—were quite similar on the old and new KIRIS scales (Table A.2).

Table A.1

Mathematics Mean NAPD Scores and Changes, Old and New KIRIS Scales

	1993	1994	Change
Grade 4			
KIRIS old scale	21.6	30.2	8.6
KIRIS new scale	22.0	34.0	12.0
Grade 8			
KIRIS old scale	25.2	33.0	7.8
KIRIS new scale	23.0	31.0	8.0

Table A.2

Grade 12 Mean NAPD Scores and Changes, Old and New KIRIS Scales

	1993	1994	Change
Mathematics			
KIRIS old scale	41.6	53.2	11.6
KIRIS new scale	38.5	51.2	12.7
Reading			
KIRIS old scale	32.5	49.5	17.0
KIRIS new scale	28.9	43.9	15.0
Science			
KIRIS old scale	34.6	42.4	7.8
KIRIS new scale	35.4	44.4	9.1

Given these similarities, a simple additive adjustment was used to create a continuous data series including 1992. In 1993 and thereafter, the new scale, which represents a better scaling method, was always used. Estimated 1992 means on the new scale were obtained by subtracting from each 1993 mean on the new scale the 1992-to-1993 change on the old scale.

STANDARDIZING KIRIS, ACT, AND NAEP TREND DATA

Test-score trends were placed on a common metric by expressing changes in terms of the variability of performance in a base year—specifically, as fractions of a standard deviation. Often, the choice of a base year for standardizing trends in this fashion is of little consequence because the standard deviation is typically quite stable over moderate periods of time. As noted in Chapter 4, however, the standard deviation of some KIRIS scores on the NAPD scale increased substantially over the first years of the program because of the decreasing concentration of scores at the lowest scale points. Standard deviations for mathematics and reading in grades 4 and 8 are shown in Table A.3 using the initial KIRIS NAPD scale and the new NAPD scale introduced in 1995 and applied retroactively. Because of these changes in the standard deviation, the choice of a year for standardization could appreciably alter the findings presented, although our major conclusions would not change.

Table A.3

Standard Deviations of KIRIS Scores, Old and New NAPD Scales

	1992	1993	1994	1995	1996
Grade 4					
Mathematics					
Old Scale	28.4	32.0	36.5		
New Scale		32.8	37.3	39.4	36.4
Reading					
Old Scale	24.4	26.8	28.8		
New Scale		27.6	26.5	32.6	32.2
Grade 8					
Mathematics					
Old Scale	36.4	42.2	44.6		
New Scale		43.4	45.5	49.5	48.2
Reading					
Old Scale	24.5	27.9	30.0		
New Scale		27.2	29.8	24.2	23.1

All of the standardizations used in comparing KIRIS scores with ACT and NAEP scores in this report are based on the 1994 standard deviations. The 1994 scores represent the midpoint of the series used in comparisons with NAEP and are near the midpoint of the ACT comparisons. In addition, this choice makes the analyses consistent with the OEA Panel analyses of NAEP and ACT data, which used 1994 standard deviations for both data series. Also, in many instances, the substantial changes in the standard deviations appear to have ended by 1994.

An important question is whether the use of standardized NAPD scores distorts the conclusions because the NAPD scale is discrete and showed rapid changes in the concentration of scores. This question cannot be answered completely for the same reason that NAPD scores were used in the analysis: theta scores are not available for 1992. However, it is possible to check the effect of using NAPD scores for the three years for which both scales were available by comparing standardized changes in mathematics, reading, and science obtained with theta and NAPD scores for that period. This was done using the ACT analysis sample described below. In that sample, the use of NAPD scores had only modest effect; gains were slightly smaller in mathematics and reading and moderately smaller in science when NADP scores were used (Table A.4). Because KIRIS scores increased much more than scores on the ACT and NAEP, the use of NAPD scores is in this case conservative, understating the discrepancy between NAPD scores and external measures.

CREATING THE KIRIS-ACT DATABASE

The databases we used to compare ACT and KIRIS scores were created by American College Testing, which merged KIRIS data to a subset of variables from their records for all Kentucky students who took the ACT. Only a student's most recent ACT scores were included in the merged database. A remerge was conducted by RAND to add to the 1993 and

Table A.4

**Standardized Gains on KIRIS for ACT Analysis
Sample, Using NAPD and Theta Scores**

	93 to 94	93 to 95
Mathematics		
NAPD scores	0.28	0.61
Theta scores	0.39	0.68
Reading		
NAPD scores	0.47	0.60
Theta scores	0.59	0.65
Science		
NAPD scores	0.34	0.55
Theta scores	0.47	0.74

1994 KIRIS-ACT databases the new NAPD and theta scores created by KDE when KDE rescaled the 1993 and 1994 KIRIS scores.

Adjusting for Differences Between Grade 11 and Grade 12

Beginning in 1995, KIRIS testing was dropped from the twelfth to the eleventh grade, which made it necessary to adjust the grade 11 scores to put them on the scale used previously for grade 12 students (or vice versa). KDE conducted a common-items equating and concluded that a simple additive adjustment to grade 11 scores was sufficient. For its purposes, KDE calculated the effect of this change on the total accountability index and adjusted the baseline for the second accountability cycle (i.e., 1993 and 1994 indices) downward accordingly (Kentucky Department of Education, 1997).

For our purposes, however, it was necessary to adjust scores in individual subject areas. It was simpler to increase the 1995 scores than to adjust all of the earlier years. Thus, all grade 11 scores from 1995 were increased by an additive constant for each subject area based on the results of the common-items equating conducted by KDE. The upward adjustments were 3.03 scale points in reading, 2.00 points in mathematics, 0.11 points in science, and 0.16 points in social studies (Kentucky Department of Education, 1997, Table 9-10, p. 9-18).

The change to grade 11 also added a delay in the availability of merged ACT-KIRIS data because many of the students who take KIRIS in their junior year will take the ACT in the following year, and two years of ACT data therefore must be used in the merge. For example, both 1994-95 and 1995-96 ACT data must be merged to the 1994-95 KIRIS data. This precluded analysis of 1996 KIRIS results here because 1996-97 ACT data were not yet available when this analysis was conducted. Since there were no mean gains in KIRIS scores in mathematics, science, or reading from 1995 to 1996 to evaluate, however, this limitation was not important.

Creating and Evaluating an Analysis Sample

A comparison of statewide trends on KIRIS and the ACT could be misleading because of the self-selection of students taking the ACT. The students who elect to take the ACT are not representative of the state's entire student population. They may have shown different trends on KIRIS. More important, the selectivity of the group taking the ACT might have changed over the years in question, biasing trends in mean scores on the ACT.

Accordingly, all our analyses compare ACT and KIRIS scores only for the students for whom scores on both tests were available. All KIRIS trends were recomputed for the subsample of students who took both tests, and these recomputed trends were then compared to trends in ACT scores. This process removes possible bias in the comparisons from changes in the selectivity of the ACT group or from other differences between ACT-takers and other students.

Because schools are the unit of accountability in KIRIS, some of our analyses focused on schools, and it was therefore necessary to exclude schools within which very few students took both KIRIS and the ACT. Accordingly, our analyses (including student-level analyses) include only students in schools in which more than ten students took both assessments and had matched records. The number of schools deleted from analysis was small in every year other than 1992, when the KIRIS database included many schools with ten or fewer students tested (Table A.5).

Table A.5

ACT Analysis Sample of Schools with More Than Ten Matched ACT and KIRIS Scores

	All schools	Analysis Sample	Percent Dropped
1992	307	229	25
1993	251	232	8
1994	242	227	6
1995	245	230	6

The analysis sample constituted half or more of the tested Kentucky student cohort in each year of the study, but the percentage varied from year to year (Table A.6). Note that despite an increase in the number of students in the sample in 1995, the percentage of students in the analysis sample dropped because the total number of students increased much more. We speculate that this increase in the total number of students reflects in large measure the switch from grade 12 to grade 11 testing, which added to the database students who would drop out between the spring of their junior year and the spring of their senior year.

Although this sampling removes potential bias in the comparisons between KIRIS and ACT scores, it also raises questions about the comparability of the analysis sample (students who took the ACT and attended a school in which more than ten students took the ACT) with the state as a whole. This question was analyzed in two stages. The first explored the comparability of trends in selected schools to trends statewide. The second stage evaluated, for students within selected schools, the similarity of KIRIS trends for students who took the ACT to KIRIS trends for all students.

Table A.6

ACT Analysis Sample as Percentage of All Students Tested with KIRIS, Reading

	All Students	Matched Students	Matched Students in Analysis Sample	Analysis Sample as Percentage of All Students
1992	35,702	18,075	18,020	50
1993[a]	35,832	20,497	20,466	57
1994	36,528	20,612	20,563	56
1995	41,469	21,352	21,301	51

[a]Counts in 1993 are students for whom scores were available on the old KIRIS NAPD scale. In 1993, fewer students had scores on the new scale on data provided by KDE. The reasons for the discrepancy could not be determined, but analysis showed that it had no appreciable impact on the conclusions.

As one would expect, the analysis sample had higher average scores than the state as a whole, particularly in mathematics (Table A.7). Perhaps more important, the subsample had greater increases on KIRIS than did the total student population. The sampling of schools had no appreciable effect; trends in the selected schools were very similar to those in the state as a whole (see Table A.8, which shows only means on the newer NAPD scale). The second stage of sampling, however, mattered more: within the selected schools, students with ACT scores tended to show larger changes in performance than all students in those schools, particularly in KIRIS mathematics (Table A.8). (The declines that occurred in

Table A.7

Mean KIRIS Scores, 1993, for All Students Statewide and All Students in Schools with More Than Ten Matched KIRIS-ACT Cases

	All Students, All Schools	Matched Students, Analysis Sample	Difference, All vs. Matched
Mathematics	26.9	38.5	11.6
Reading	21.3	28.9	7.6
Science	28.6	35.4	6.8

Table A.8

1993-1995 Changes in Mean KIRIS Scores for All Students Statewide and All Students in Schools with More Than Ten Matched KIRIS-ACT Cases

	All Students, All Schools	All Students in Analysis Sample of Schools	Matched Students in Analysis Sample of Schools	Percent Difference, Matched vs. All
Mathematics	21.5	20.7	27.7	+29
Reading	15.4	15.6	19.1	+24
Science	12.3	12.5	14.8	+20

NOTE: Changes incorporate equating adjustment to place 1995 grade 11 scores on the scale of previous grade 12 scores.

KIRIS reading and science scores between 1992 and 1993, not shown in Table A.8, were also somewhat larger in the subsample of students that took the ACT.)

Evaluating Anomalous Scores in 1994

As noted in Chapter 8, the 1994 KIRIS scores appear anomalous in some respects. KIRIS scores correlated less with ACT scores in 1994 than in any other year, and the distribution of theta scores appeared to be somewhat atypical (with more compression of scores at the low end). This anomaly appeared with old NAPD scores, new (rescaled) NAPD scores, and theta scores. No explanation of this anomaly has been identified. For this reason, no conclusions that would depend on the anomalous characteristics of 1994 scores are presented.

REFERENCES

Advanced Systems for Measurement in Education (1995). Unpublished item scoring rubric. Dover, NH: author.

American College Testing (1989). *Preliminary Technical Manual for the Enhanced ACT Assessment.* Iowa City: author.

American College Testing (1996). *ACT English Test.* http://www.act.org/aap/STRAT/EnglishStrats.html (March 1).

Beaton, A. E., Mullis, I. V. S., Martin, M. O., Gonzalez, E. J., Kelly, D. L., and Smith, T. A. (1996). *Mathematics Achievement in the Middle School Years.* Chestnut Hill, MA: TIMSS International Study Center, Boston College.

Beaton, A. E., Zwick, R., Yamamoto, K., Mislevy, R. J., Johnson, E. G., and Rust, K. F. (1990). *Disentangling the NAEP 1985-86 Reading Anomaly.* Princeton: National Assessment of Educational Progress/Educational Testing Service.

Berends, M., and Koretz, D. (1996). Reporting minority students' test scores: How well can the National Assessment of Educational Progress account for differences in social context? *Educational Assessment, 3*(3), 249-285.

Bond, L., and Jaeger, R. M. (1993). Judged congruence between various state assessment tests in mathematics and the 1990 National Assessment of Educational Progress Item Pool for Grade-8 Mathematics. In National Academy of Education, *The Trial State Assessment: Prospects and Realities: Background Studies.* Stanford: National Academy of Education, Stanford University, 401-478.

Catterall, J. S., Mehrens, W. A., Ryan, J. M., Flores, E. J., and Rubin, P. M. (1998). *Kentucky Instructional Results Information System: A Technical Review.* Frankfort, KY: Kentucky Legislative Research Commission, January.

Durbin, A. (1998). Personal communication, January 6.

Hambleton, R. K. (1989). Principles and selected applications of item response theory. In R. L. Linn (Ed.), *Educational Measurement, Third Edition.* New York: American Council on Education and Macmillan Publishing Company, 147-200.

Hambleton, R. K., Jaeger, R. M., Koretz, D., Linn, R. L., Millman, J., and Phillips, S. E. (1995). *Review of the Measurement Quality of the Kentucky Instructional Results Information System, 1991-1994.* Frankfort: Office of Education Accountability, Kentucky General Assembly, June.

Haertel, E., Forgione, P. D., Walberg, H. J., Baldwin, J., Bock, R. D., Burstein, L., Carlson, D., Chall, J. S., Guthrie, J. T., Hedges, L. V., Melnick, D., Musick, M. D., Pandey, T., Schmidt, W. H., and Wiley, D. E. (1989). *Report of the NAEP Technical Review Panel on the 1986 Reading Anomaly, the Accuracy of NAEP Trends, and Issues Raised by State-Level NAEP Comparisons.* Washington, D.C.: National Center for Education Statistics (CS 89-499).

Hoffman, G. (1997). Personal communication, December 18.

Kentucky Department of Education (1993a). *Kentucky Instructional Results Information System, 1991-92 Technical Report*. Frankfort, KY: author.

Kentucky Department of Education (1993b). *Transformations: Kentucky's Curriculum Framework*. Frankfort, KY: author.

Kentucky Department of Education (1994). *Kentucky Instructional Results Information System, 1992-93 Technical Report*. Frankfort, KY: author.

Kentucky Department of Education (1995a). *Celebrate the Progress! 1992-1994 Kentucky Accountability Results Summary News Packet*. Frankfort, KY: author, February 7.

Kentucky Department of Education (1995b). *KIRIS Accountability Cycle 1 Technical Manual*. Frankfort, KY: author.

Kentucky Department of Education (1995c). *Transformations: Kentucky's Curriculum Framework* (revised version). Frankfort, KY: author.

Kentucky Department of Education (1996a). *1996 Writing Audit: Final Report*. Frankfort, KY: author, September 23.

Kentucky Department of Education (1996b). *Kentucky School and District Accountability Results, Accountability Cycle 2: Briefing Packet*. Frankfort, KY: author.

Kentucky Department of Education (1996c). *Core Content for Assessment*. Frankfort, KY: author.

Kentucky Department of Education (1997). *KIRIS Accountability Cycle 2 Technical Manual*. Frankfort, KY: author.

Koretz, D. (1986). *Trends in Educational Achievement*. Washington, D.C.: Congressional Budget Office.

Koretz, D. (1987). *Educational Achievement: Explanations and Implications of Recent Trends*. Washington, D.C.: Congressional Budget Office.

Koretz, D. (1996). Using student assessments for educational accountability. In R. Hanushek (Ed.), *Improving the Performance of America's Schools*. Washington, D.C.: National Academy Press, 171-196.

Koretz, D. (1997). *The Assessment of Students with Disabilities in Kentucky*. Los Angeles: Center for Research on Evaluation, Standards, and Student Testing, UCLA (CSE Technical Report 431).

Koretz, D., Barron, S., Mitchell, K., and Stecher, B. (1996). *The Perceived Effects of the Kentucky Instructional Results Information System (KIRIS)*. Santa Monica: RAND (MR-792-PCT/FF).

Koretz, D., Linn, R. L., Dunbar, S. B., and Shepard, L. A. (1991). The effects of high-stakes testing: Preliminary evidence about generalization across tests. In R. L. Linn (chair), *The*

Effects of High Stakes Testing, symposium presented at the annual meetings of the American Educational Research Association and the National Council on Measurement in Education, Chicago, April.

Koretz, D., Mitchell, K., Barron, S., and Keith, S. (1996). *The Perceived Effects of the Maryland School Performance Assessment Program.* Los Angeles: Center for the Study of Evaluation, University of California (CSE Technical Report No. 409).

Linn, R. L. (1993). Linking results of distinct assessments. *Applied Measurement in Education, 6*(1), 83-102.

Linn, R. L. (1997). Personal communication, October 3.

Mislevy, R. J. (1992). Scaling procedures. In E. G. Johnson and N. L. Allen (Eds.), *The NAEP 1990 Technical Report.* Washington: National Center for Education Statistics (Report 21-TR-20).

Nitko, A. J., Stone, C. A., and Wang, Shudong (1997). Patterns of school achievement: A comparison of KIRIS and standardized achievement test results over time in selected Kentucky schools. Pittsburgh: School of Education, University of Pittsburgh, unpublished manuscript.

Reese, C. M., Miller, K. E., Mazzeo, J., and Dossey, J. A. (1997). *NAEP 1996 Mathematics Report Card for the Nation and the States.* Washington: National Center for Education Statistics.

Stecher, B. M., and Mitchell, K. J. (1995). *Portfolio Driven Reform: Vermont Teachers' Understanding of Mathematical Problem-Solving.* Los Angeles, CA: Center for Research on Evaluation, Standards, and Student Testing (CSE Technical Report 400).

Zlatos, W. (1994). Running up the score. *In Pittsburgh*, March.